WHOLELINESS

ALSO BY CARMEN HARRA, Ph.D.

Decoding Your Destiny

The Eleven Eternal Principles: Accessing the Divine Within

Everyday Karma: A Renowned Psychic Shows You
How to Change Your Life by Changing Your Karma

Signs, Symbols and Secrets: Decoding the Da Vinci Code

The Trinity of Health: Align Body, Mind and Soul
in Order to Achieve Health and Happiness for Your Whole Life

Please visit:

Hay House USA: **www.hayhouse.com**®
Hay House Australia: **www.hayhouse.com.au**
Hay House UK: **www.hayhouse.co.uk**
Hay House South Africa: **www.hayhouse.co.za**
Hay House India: **www.hayhouse.co.in**

WHOLELINESS

Embracing
the Sacred Unity
That Heals Our World

CARMEN HARRA, Ph.D.

HAY HOUSE, INC.
Carlsbad, California • New York City
London • Sydney • Johannesburg
Vancouver • Hong Kong • New Delhi

Published and distributed in the United States by: Hay House, Inc.: www.hayhouse .com • *Published and distributed in Australia by:* Hay House Australia Pty. Ltd.: www.hayhouse.com.au • *Published and distributed in the United Kingdom by:* Hay House UK, Ltd.: www.hayhouse.co.uk • *Published and distributed in the Republic of South Africa by:* Hay House SA (Pty), Ltd.: www.hayhouse.co.za • *Distributed in Canada by:* Raincoast: www.raincoast.com • *Published in India by:* Hay House Publishers India: www.hayhouse.co.in

Project editor: Patrick Gabrysiak
Cover design: Christy Salinas • *Interior design:* Charles McStravick

Library of Congress Cataloging-in-Publication Data

Harra, Carmen.
  Wholeliness : embracing the sacred unity that heals our world / Carmen Harra. -- 1st ed.
    p. cm.
  ISBN 978-1-4019-3144-5 (tradepaper : alk. paper) 1. Change (Psychology) 2. Change (Psychology)--Religious aspects. 3. Spirituality. I. Title.
  BF637.C4H359 2011
  158--dc22

                              2010052866

Tradepaper ISBN: 978-1-4019-3144-5
Digital ISBN: 978-1-4019-3145-2

14 13 12 11   4 3 2
1st edition, May 2011

Printed in the United States of America

I dedicate this book

to my husband, Virgil;

my mother, Sanda;

and my father, Victor:

my three guardian angels.

CONTENTS

Editor's Note: In order to avoid awkward "he/she," "him/her" references, either masculine or feminine pronouns have been used for certain examples, alternating between the two. Please note that all of the information within this book applies universally to both men and women.

WHAT IS WHOLELINESS?
A DEFINITION

whole·li·ness \HOL-lee-ness\ *n*. The condition, state, or quality
of being healed, whole, and in harmony with the Divine and all that exists.
From the Old English word *hal,* meaning "healthy, unhurt, entire." (*Hal* is
also the root word for *holy,* which means "saintly, godly, or spiritually pure.")

When our minds create the illusion of separateness, we forget that our true nature, and the nature of the universe itself, is wholeliness.

Wholeliness is the antidote to human suffering. As long as our souls inhabit human bodies, we can experience this quality only briefly. When our souls detach from our bodies and we return to consciousness, however, we come back to a natural state of wholeliness.

As human beings, we can experience wholeliness when we recognize and cherish our sacred connections to other people; the earth; the universe; and the past, present, and future. When we release the illusion of separateness and discord that our minds have created, we remember our true nature and feel in our hearts that we are not alone or disconnected after all. We perceive that we are whole and perfect just as we are, that there is harmony in the universe, and that darkness must exist along with the light to complete the whole. We understand that it is our natural state to enjoy health, experience the perfection of harmony, and be immersed in Spirit—yet also be aware of ourselves as individual, glorious expressions of the Divine Force.

We feel compelled to manifest wholeliness so that others may feel the comfort, joy, and force of these sacred connections; and we *will* find the courage to create wellness, balance, and cooperation on Earth.

When we believe in the power of wholeliness and choose to manifest it as often as possible, we live with purpose, knowing that each of us plays a vital role in the healing of a world that has become unbalanced and disharmonious. Despite our challenges, this faith in our ability to achieve wholeliness allows us to be at peace with that which we cannot change, and to accept with awe the mystery and complexity of our human existence. Optimism, creativity, and hope thrive as we choose wholeliness over the illusion of separation.

Wholeliness is the balm that our world desperately needs at this moment as we undergo an evolution in human consciousness.

· · ● · ·

PREFACE

If I close my eyes, I can see it all again: The plump summer tomatoes were ripening off to the far left side of my grandmother's large and fertile country garden. She bent over to collect a few of the biggest ones as several chickens waddled past. Inside the house, my younger sister sat at the wooden dining table peeling newly picked potatoes with a knife. *Just a few hours,* I thought with a smile, *and they'll all be here.* I sprinted through that lovely garden to help my grandmother, in preparation for our family dinner.

Later, my entire family gathered around the wooden table, joined in each other's presence, just as simple meals have been shared by countless families and friends for centuries. To laugh without restraint and eat freshly prepared food, to spread the joy of loving company and reassure each other that we would always remain united through the ebb and flow of life—this was all we needed. We spoke boisterously yet warmly, bellowing jokes across the table. No one uttered a word of complaint that we couldn't afford a television set for our minuscule house located far from the bustle of the city. No mention was made of the extreme Communist regime that often rendered our supermarkets so empty that our faces reflected in the barren steel shelves. We simply absorbed the rustic ambience of our home and the peace it delivered to our souls as we raised our glasses in a uniform toast of high and low voices: "To family."

In terms of material wealth, we were extremely poor. We had no running water, and my sister and I were careful with our few precious toys, supplementing them with items we found in the woods and the figments of our rich imaginations. Despite our poverty, we felt rich in our ability to lift each other up through any phase of life. From a very young age, we knew what mattered.

• • •

As a little girl, I was convinced that I would be a great singer and appear on television someday. Despite having spent a year in the hospital due to asthma, I developed such a powerful voice that I was able to win one singing contest after another. Then, as I entered my teenage years, I began to rise to fame. By the time I was 27, I had released 12 albums and was a household name in my country. My singing career allowed me to help my family financially: I carried them on my shoulders with great pleasure, as they had always supported me.

When I left Romania behind and immigrated to America, I cried, not knowing when I'd be able to see everyone again. Having given up my homeland for the West, I wouldn't be welcomed back—the Iron Curtain stood between me and those I loved. But I was fortunate enough to find my husband very soon after arriving in the U.S.; I was even luckier that he, too, came from a large, welcoming family. They were always there for one another, celebrating every special occasion and coming together in times of difficulty, much like what I'd just left behind.

My husband and I also started a family of our own and raised three daughters. But today, not only do I find myself without my parents, but my husband, Virgil, recently passed away from lung cancer. Only after life had taken away so many of the people I love did I realize just how much more empowered I felt when my family was *whole*. As with any family, we had our squabbles, but with so little to distract us or fool us into believing that possessions would make us happy, we always came together again in forgiveness. We were the source of each other's strength and resilience. There was always someone to listen when we were feeling scared or sad, someone to lend support and gently remind us to return our thoughts to all that is beautiful in life—to joy and optimism.

• • •

The delicious food at my childhood home's wooden table sustained us, but it was the company that gave us vitality and hope. Now I meet many people who have luxurious homes with expensive, quality sets of fine china in ornate dining rooms, as well as access to produce from thousands of miles away and 24-hour grocery stores filled with all they could ever want to eat. They have families and neighbors and know many more people, yet they feel lonely and disconnected. They often sit alone with their worries, certain that no one else would understand, convinced that friends and family would be far too busy to listen to their troubles . . . so they remain silent and detached.

When you sit around a table with others, you restore your strength. You nourish yourself with the fruit of the earth, as well as with laughter, love, conversation, and memories. If you pay close attention, you start to become aware of your connections to those who came before you and those who will come after you— to those you may never meet but who, like you, gather around the table.

You are part of a large family called the human race. Peace and power are yours when you realize that you're never alone—that you're always loved, heard, valued, and supported. This knowledge will give you the courage to believe in tomorrow and keep pressing forward, even when the road is treacherous and the path in front of you isn't clear. That is the power of wholeliness.

Wholeliness in Difficult Times

Wholeliness can help you overcome any adversity, as it has done for me. It's brought me through the worst of times, and it's also inspired me to share this gift of knowing that love and strength are always present within.

All people live through moments so cruel that they actually begin to question the reason for their existence on Earth. Life delivers sheer joy, but it also brings forth repeated bouts of misfortune. My own life, like anyone else's, has not been short of tragic moments; in fact, Virgil's recent death was the most devastating event I've ever been through.

When I lost my husband after 27 years of marriage, I felt as if the breath had been sucked out of me and my soul had been shattered. In the beginning, not a day went by that I didn't question why he had been taken from me. I had trouble eating, sleeping, and functioning overall. As this dragged on, I noticed that my broken heart wasn't healing.

Then I acknowledged that perhaps I needed help. My heart couldn't heal on its own, and I wasn't about to just sit around and wait until the aching went away. I foresaw that the pain wouldn't leave my mind and body unless I did my best to push it out by drawing on the strength of all the love surrounding me.

And so I turned, as I often do, to wholeliness as a method of healing: I began to pray intensely to God and my guardian angels to help me return to my natural state of wholeliness, and to show me what I needed to know and do. Whenever I was about to cry, I let myself feel the knot in my throat but consciously chose not to generate thoughts that would disempower me and create more sorrow. Instead, I'd start praying so that I would experience my sacred connection to Spirit.

I also sought methods of relaxation, finding that deep breathing, exercising, and walking in nature were very helpful. I allowed the sun to breathe its warm light upon me. I stopped to admire every flower, and I observed every creature in its natural habitat. In this way, I made myself aware of the grandeur of the world and was able to momentarily step out of my own personal dilemma and into a brief but nourishing state of wholeliness.

I also started scribbling down my feelings: my frustration, sadness, and anger. I released these emotions from my body through my hand as it passionately wrote. Through this practice, God was showing me the reasons for my husband's passing, and I began to comprehend the greater purpose of this tragedy. I didn't fight it; rather, I allowed God to show me what I needed to see in order to regain peace. I absorbed that peace and moved toward acceptance.

Most of all, I contacted and communicated with my husband on a daily basis. Whether he leaned over my bedside to embrace me longingly in one of those entrancing dreams from which no one wishes to wake, or used hints to reveal his presence (by repeatedly flipping on a light switch in the middle of the day, let's say), he made me aware of his energy.

I also often felt his presence forcefully. He frequently said that just as he hadn't wanted to depart the earth, he didn't want to leave me now. This made my melancholy more bitter, yet Virgil's message also caressed my soul in some inexplicable way. I knew better than to think that this was the end, or that I would never see or hear him again.

And so, through a combination of wholeliness, faith, and time, I was slowly able to overcome my deep sorrow. As the proverb says: "This, too, shall pass."

Even though I sometimes asked myself, "How can I go on?" deep down I knew what I needed to do because of what I'd already experienced in my life. I needed to return myself to a state of wholeliness and trust in the power of the sacred healing connections to others, God, and the universe. These connections always served to bring about courage and faith, and had never before failed to keep me afloat as I navigated my way through loss and transition.

It was time to say good-bye to the old and step into the unknown, as I'd done time and time again. I'd always found it helpful to take part in certain practices—such as praying and sharing meals with others—that connected me to wholeliness and helped me reject the idea that life is a constant struggle for survival.

Redefining My Life

As a result of my intuitive gifts, which I acquired after nearly drowning as a small child, I'm able to access the great collective consciousness, where information about the past, present, and future can be found. I can "see" intelligence that's invisible to those who aren't as intuitive (although I believe that everyone has this gift to some degree). By using these abilities, I was able to see that the best way to heal is to acknowledge and make use of sacred connections. After Virgil died, I drew upon the love and strength I received from God, Who is ever present. I remained in communication with my husband, despite his transition to a being without physical form, and I never doubted that I'd always be in contact with him.

I also opened up to friends and family members, as well as sought help from others who showed great compassion for those who were suffering. Again and again, I'd encounter the individuals who would provide just the right encouragement and support exactly when I needed it. Often such meetings seemed coincidental, but because of my ability to predict such connections, I became aware that they were part of a larger plan that God has for us to experience healing, joy, and love. I knew that however dark my life was at that moment, love and happiness would return, inspired by people I was meant to know in this lifetime.

It was clear that I had to nurture my body, mind, and spirit for the sake of my health and well-being. As an intuitive, I'd observed dark energies lodged in people's etheric bodies, which surround the physical body (I'll explain more about this later), many times; and I'd witnessed how they went on to develop an imbalance, tumor, or ailment in the physical region that was aligned with dark areas in the etheric body.

I was aware that my own deep grief might cause me to develop a cold or heavy areas of energy in my own etheric body that could manifest in illness. I also knew that the sacred connections between mind, body, and spirit are ones that can cause suffering or healing at every level, depending on the choices we make. Anything I did to improve my mood, make my thoughts more positive, or lift my spirits would help me avoid illness and additional anguish.

I made the choice to reject the cynical notion that life is a constant struggle for survival; instead, I trusted in the healing that would surely come to me through my relationship with God, the universe, other people, spirits, and all creatures on the planet. Whenever I started to feel myself giving in to despair, I recognized how this would affect me and consciously focused on achieving wholeliness—the state of peace and power that comes from being a conduit of love, strength, and courage for the Divine Creator.

Believe me, it took mental discipline to stay positive. I reminded myself that when joyous events occur, they're always accompanied by some sort of loss, and vice versa. Often, I thought back to when I'd left Europe and gotten married. Because of my choice, I'd had to leave behind the only life I knew: gain and loss were intertwined. And as much as I loved my new life, it became clear that my singing career might never be the same in America. Instead of dwelling on that loss, I got a day job and began expressing myself through making jewelry as well as music.

Soon after I redefined myself in the United States, I also started to work as an intuitive counselor and began to help friends and co-workers. It didn't occur to me that this might lead to a new career that would eventually involve writing books and appearing on television. In fact, at first I didn't even think to charge money for what I was doing! I recall my very first session with the actress Candice Bergen, who had heard of me through friends of hers. She came to my office, and I told her about a physical ailment her daughter was experiencing and reassured her that the child would be fine as long as she had surgery. Candice was shocked, as she hadn't told anyone this terrible news. But she was much relieved by my prediction (which did come true). She asked how much she owed me, and I said, "I don't know . . . $20?"

Just like that, the next step on my journey was to provide people with professional help through my insights. My intuitive mind has helped me "read" individuals and pinpoint their problems, but only through my knowledge of cognitive therapy have I been able to create profound and powerful methods of healing. I have guided my clients in the right direction by utilizing both my God-given skills and what I've learned. (It is interesting to note that many of those who seek the help of an intuitive are quite disturbed and actually have clinical problems. This is why intuitive guidance alone is insufficient in giving them the help they need. I've always believed that psychological components coupled with the abilities of my intuitive mind are the reason I've been able to assist people of all walks of life. I also believe that psychology today should expand to accept ancient teachings, and even para-psychology, as tools to better understand human behavior.)

What Wholeliness Has Meant for My Life

So often in my life I've had to start over, and as a result have felt confused, disoriented, and scared. Because of my ability to see my sacred connections to God—Who works through people, nature, the stars, the sun, coincidence, and many different tools to bring love and healing to us all—I've always been able to eventually let go of the old and embrace the new. Thanks to a sense of wholeliness, I have a great appreciation for all the gifts in my life, for all those who have encouraged me or offered me opportunities to better my situation.

I've developed the habit of saying "I love you" whenever I talk to people, because I recognize that I *do* love everyone, and all of us need to be reminded of the love that's available at all times. I truly want to help those who support me in any way, even if it's just by expressing caring and gratitude and attempting to make the world a better place.

I trust in God and follow the path that is being laid out for me. I believe that for anything I leave behind, something as good, if not better, will appear in my future—that's because I consciously do my best to resolve the karma that could attract situations of sorrow, fear, or resentment to me. In short, whatever losses I've experienced have been balanced by growth, new opportunities, and a deeper faith that the Divine takes care of us all. The connection between *loss* and *gain* is not lost on me.

Throughout my life, I've stayed connected to God. Although I continue to practice the faith of my childhood (orthodox Christianity), I also recognize that religion can divide us, while spirituality brings us together. I'm able to feel the peace, power, healing, and sense of completeness and perfection that come from wholeliness. I believe that when Jesus said, "I and the Father are one," he meant that there is no division between the Creator and creation, which includes the human race. Even science is beginning to recognize the formerly hidden connections that bind us to each other and the cosmos. "Split the wood, and I am there," Jesus said. The Divine Force is everywhere, in all of us, enveloping everyone and everything with the sweeping energy of love.

I know that I am not just one person struggling to find happiness despite the turbulence in my life. I, like you, am part of a much larger whole that is boundless in its love and support. I see this in my work when I access hidden information about the past, present, and future. I trust in the power of these invisible, sacred relationships, which our troubled world is far too quick to deny. Whenever it seems dark, I embrace the idea of unity that offers peace and hope—I try to create a state of wholeliness in my life and the larger world.

For example, my belief in this concept inspired me to not just make music, but to sing from the depths of my heart so that I might move others to feel the happiness and hope that I do. In turn, this inspired me to create jewelry that incorporated spiritual symbolism, so that the wearer would feel connected whenever she looked at or touched one of these powerful objects. And wholeliness expanded my thinking so that I could recognize my need to develop new skills and techniques to help those for whom I was giving sessions.

Years ago, I earned a Ph.D. in hypnotherapy and another in psychology and went on to become a clinical psychologist, in the hopes that I might be of even greater service to those who came to me. Whatever success I've experienced, I know it's always meant to push me toward doing even more to help others. It's clear that my purpose here on Earth is to help the material realm more closely mirror that which is beyond the physical senses: the realm of Spirit, where healing, wholeness, and well-being are the natural states of existence.

I know in my heart that every member of the human race has a purpose that involves bringing wholeliness into the world. Humanity is a large family that has its conflicts and disagreements, but if we can let go of our fears and insecurities, we can see past them and discover our unique purpose. We can begin to value the love in our lives that's always available to us. Whenever I see my late husband's family, it's a reunion—I'm reminded that although some people no longer sit at the table in corporeal form, they are still there, and new ones are joining us all the time. And so it is with the human family.

From this table, where we break bread and speak with love to each other, we go forth into the world and manifest wholeliness in every way we can. Together, we find solutions to our problems and invent new and even better ways of working and living together. We rediscover our enormous capacity for love, creation, and harmony; and, filled with enthusiasm, we press forward in our collective evolution.

It's an honor to be a part of this family and share with you what I have learned about wholeliness.

— **Carmen Harra, Ph.D.**
Hollywood, Florida

· · ● · ·

INTRODUCTION

Your eyes tell you that human beings are separate creatures with distinct bodies, minds, ideas, personalities, and lifestyles. Even so, there may have been a moment when you became aware that all is not as it seems, that there are connections that can't be perceived with the senses, and that we are each a part of a greater entity. This moment may have been fleeting, and it could have occurred so long ago that you doubt your memory of it. Perhaps you dismissed its importance afterward because you didn't know what to make of such a mysterious experience of unity with all creation.

Or maybe you'd like to think that we are all connected as part of one family that's in harmony with all that exists, but the suffering you see in this world, or the pain you experience when you lose someone you love, is so strong that you find it hard to believe in anything but chaos and randomness.

Yet there is a fabric of reality—a hidden order that lies underneath the world of sight, sound, and smell. You can't see it or run your fingers over it, but it's there. You sense it when you're aware of strange coincidences that defy logic and the laws of probability, or when you somehow—inexplicably—know for certain that you and a particular person will be married one day, even though you just met. And you perceive this connection when the impossible suddenly becomes possible and your heart tells you that Divine intervention has occurred.

Your soul recognizes this other, greater reality beyond the senses . . . but your head denies it. If you've ever had the opportunity to glimpse the greater reality, your mind may have dismissed it because it couldn't understand, control, or conform to the truth. In frustration, you may have convinced yourself that it wasn't "real" after all. However, as the science of quantum mechanics begins to reveal hints of that hidden reality, perhaps your logical mind will start to listen to what your soul is whispering: *There's more to life than suffering and struggle. And there is a meaning you aren't perceiving.*

Whenever we read about the ancient teachings of philosophers, prophets, shamans, and spiritual leaders, the beauty and truth of their words awaken in us the awareness that these wise beings knew something that we seem to have forgotten. They were fully conscious of the exquisite fabric that weaves us all together in a reality that defies the restrictions of the material world.

This reality is information and awareness. It is pure Divine love and the light of consciousness; it is the framework of creation itself that is ever evolving, becoming brighter and causing the darkness of ignorance, fear, anger, war, suffering, and disease to dissipate. It is the "whole" of which each of us is a tiny piece—it is a quilt of many colors. It is Divine, and it exists according to its own laws.

As I explained in my book *The Eleven Eternal Principles*, the world you can touch, smell, taste, hear, and see seems so real that it's easy to become oblivious to the nature of the sacred reality lying beyond your physical senses. Instead of aligning yourself with the sacred laws, you have followed those created by human beings. You've contributed to your family, workplace, and circle of friends by doing your best to obey the rules even when it's challenging to do so. And yet, like everyone, you've known loss, pain, and injustice.

In response to the suffering we've all experienced, the human race has created inferior standards upon which we've built institutions and systems that we thought would last forever. We've used our minds to figure out how this physical world works, and how to manipulate it to better our chances of survival, happiness, and freedom. For a long time, it seemed as if our human-made laws did a pretty good job of guiding us away from hardship and toward a path of joy and fulfillment. But now we can't help thinking about all the problems that threaten to overwhelm us despite our best efforts to solve them. How many people have been—and continue to be—killed, tormented, or enslaved? Even worse, how many of these atrocities have been committed in the name of God and religion? Our systems, rules, and laws aren't working. We all know it. So why are countless problems not only continuing to plague us, but getting worse in many cases?

The earth and the heavens are crying out for us to let go of our denial and fear and find the courage to evolve in our awareness. It's time to heal the suffering we've caused, to come back to the state of being we're meant to experience. It's time to return to aligning with the law of totality, which declares that we are all one, united in the reality that lies beyond the senses.

You and the Whole

Are you an individual, or part of a larger whole? You are *both,* depending on how you choose to look at it.

Embodying the law of totality doesn't mean losing all sense of yourself as an individual. (Actually, that would be impossible.) It means embracing your dual identity as an individual *and* part of the whole. It means letting go of the illusion that the world of your senses is the only reality—an illusion that has caused too much suffering for far too long.

The problem is that it's easy to focus on your separateness rather than on your sacred connection. This distorted self-image is the root of discord in your life. It has also contributed to imbalance in the world, even if you're not aware that you have, in your own small way, played a role in creating disharmony.

The human focus on individuality and the "my group versus your group" mentality has brought us to the brink of catastrophe, to the moment in human history when the ancients prophesied that there would be a turning point. If we can admit how destructive our fear has been and reject the dominance of the ego, there is great hope for us. We don't have to experience amnesia of the soul any longer.

We've forgotten that we're not just individual, mortal beings, but eternal entities interwoven into the fabric of creation, ever connected to the loving force of the Divine. We can claim our sacred birthright: pure joy, serenity, health, and well-being. We can do this by embracing wholeliness.

Wholeliness and the Sacred Whole

For the most part, the word *holy* has been reserved for religious leaders, ceremonies, and rites. But we need to keep in mind that we are *all* blessed and in sacred unity with the whole of creation, and we don't need to receive permission from any other person to have this relationship with Spirit. We must never fear that we're not good enough to be holy. As Marianne Williamson wrote in *A Return to Love:*

> There's nothing enlightened about shrinking so that other people won't feel insecure around you. We are all meant to shine, as children do. We were born to make manifest the glory of God that is within us. It's not just in some of us; it's in everyone. And as we let our own light shine, we unconsciously give other people permission to do the same. As we are liberated from our own fear, our presence automatically liberates others.

Thinking that you're *all*-important or *un*important is an illusion created by the ego; either belief leads you away from awareness of your unity with all creation, and toward suffering and isolation.

Making your connection to the all-loving, all-powerful, Divine Force that is God will fill you with awe and is deeply healing. Enter into wholeliness and, instead of being lonely, you'll know that you belong. You'll feel loved and supported. You'll no longer sense that something is missing from your life or let your troubles overwhelm you. You'll see that you are part of a huge, loving, compassionate whole that is always pouring its nurturing, healing energy into you. You'll experience well-being on every level—physical, mental, emotional, and spiritual. Joy will fill your soul.

Understand that at first, this sensation may not last for very long before it slips away again. But you can believe in its power, that it is the natural state of both the world and *you*. And you can strive to experience wholeliness so that it continues to manifest all around you.

We must be aware, though, that suffering is part of the human condition—but it doesn't have to be central to our existence. As each of us embraces wholeliness, soon conflict, disease, and unhappiness will become scarce. We can strive to achieve perfection, a state of complete and total healing. The closer we come to manifesting wholeliness in this world, the happier we will be. It is our birthright to live in this glory—not to be plagued by discord, disease, or imbalance.

How to Use This Book

Within these pages, you'll learn how to integrate wholeliness into your life, as well as how to perceive the sacred connections that support and sustain you. You'll find out why it's so difficult for you to let go of your ego's fear of losing power—and then you'll come to understand that you absolutely can trust in God, other people, and the forces of creation to support and nurture you. You'll feel your fears subside, and your courage and faith build, as you start to identify with your true nature and your relationship to the whole. You'll also discover that in human history (and in your own), wisdom became lost when the ego took over. You can reclaim that Divine intelligence and begin healing yourself and, by extension, the entirety of humanity.

The book is organized as follows:

- In **Part I**, you'll come to see how you hold yourself back from wholeliness and why it is so urgent that you choose to evolve your consciousness.

- Then, in each chapter of **Part II**, you'll gain insight into an aspect of wholeliness and the sacred connections you've learned to overlook.

- In **Part III**, you'll face the challenging task of making two crucial shifts in perspective that will help you in your quest to achieve wholeliness: (1) adopting a new view of time; and (2) embracing a new view of religion, science, and spirituality. In the process, you'll learn how to let go of many of the limited ideas you've been taught.

- Finally, in **Part IV**, you'll discover practical ways to bring the idea of wholeliness into the world through changing your thought processes and interacting with others to help them become less divisive and feel more connected and cherished.

In each chapter, you'll be given three tasks: (1) to *observe* something about yourself and your experiences, (2) to *pray* to the Divine for assistance, and (3) to *act* in order to manifest wholeliness. Each of these efforts—observe, pray, and act—is important and effective for the evolution of humankind and the healing of all suffering, including your own.

Observe

It takes courage to be mindful and really take in everything that's happening in the present moment. Your reality right now might feel very uncomfortable, even scary. Maybe you don't know what to do to make it better. When you take the time to observe where you are, you might notice that you're in a process of change, since we are all continually transforming. Evolution is part of life, but your ego will cause you to fear it and resist it with great force.

The desire to deny what's happening is understandable, but denial doesn't work for very long. It only delays your suffering and then makes matters worse. I'll show you how you can find the courage to observe the present moment and begin to reflect upon it. This will be easier to do when you know that there's Divine support available to you and always an action you can take.

Pray

The word *pray* derives from the Latin *precari,* which means "to ask earnestly or beg." A prayer is simply a conversation with the Divine in which you ask for something to come true. Some people are very comfortable praying to God or a Higher Power, while others bristle at this or the thought of an all-powerful Creator that grants favors if you ask earnestly.

Perhaps you feel hurt, irritated, or distrustful when you think of prayer because you associate it with flawed people who misunderstand its purpose and have used it to isolate and separate humanity. Prayer is not about separation, but union. It's not about begging a powerful, fickle God to do something you want Him to do. Prayer is about connecting to the infinite, holy Source that you're a part of; asking for assistance; and opening up to this help in whatever form it is meant to come to you. Your prayers will be answered, but not always when or how you'd expect them to be. As you make a habit of praying, you'll be better able to see that this is true. In the process, you'll gain clarity about what kind of assistance you need and remind yourself that you deserve support.

If you have difficulty accepting the idea of receiving support from the Source of all creation, I ask that you continue reading. I believe that as you do, you'll feel some of that distrust and discomfort begin to melt away. You don't have to think of this energy as male or female, or as a parental figure, if that doesn't sit well with you. You might think of it as the Force of all love and understanding, infinitely compassionate and caring. I use the terms *God, Spirit,* and *the Divine* to refer to it, but I encourage you to use any word or phrase that makes you feel comfortable.

In this book, you'll learn ways in which you can actually experience your sacred connection to this Divine Force and assuage the great fear that God isn't there for you. At the end of each chapter, I'll suggest what you might pray for in order to better understand and accept an important aspect of wholeliness—whether it's of mind, body, and spirit; cosmic wholeliness; or any other form.

Act

Although you've probably heard that intent, or intention, is very important for manifesting and attracting what you desire, you must take physical action as well. When Gandhi said, "Be the change you wish to see in the world," he meant that you need to embody peace, meditate on it, and commit to it. He also meant that when faced with a potential conflict, you must choose to act peacefully. You're not "being" the change you wish to see if you give in to your ego's fear and begin fighting with others. Transformation of the external world must start within.

Action is always an important part of change. You alter thoughts and patterns of behavior only when you decide that you want to do so and take action. Although your efforts may seem small in the moment, know that many small actions form a wave of momentum.

● ● ●

This trinity of practices will help you actually feel in your heart, mind, body, and spirit that you're both an individual and a part of the whole, and therefore are in harmony with all beings and the Divine. I'll explain why this individual experience—that is, feeling and recognizing the true nature of yourself and reality itself—fosters your own healing and growth as well as the healing and evolution of all humankind.

Please believe me: your role in the fabric of the whole is utterly crucial! Humanity is at a crisis point and needs every ounce of courage, wisdom, and strength it can gather in order to evolve to a higher consciousness. You can help by bringing joy and peace into your sphere of influence as your purpose and destiny are revealed. This is all possible by embracing wholeliness and making it a part of your world. How wonderful is it that by making your own life better, you contribute to the well-being and joy of all?

The Importance of Discipline

To experience wholeliness, it's not enough to think about what you ought to do to meet the challenges you face. You must make a conscious decision to discipline your mind and change your way of perceiving so that your heart and soul open to the tremendous love, power, and wisdom of the Divine. To choose wholeliness instead of the illusion of separateness takes commitment, because the illusions of the material world are very strong.

At first, you may be frustrated by how easy it is to revert to the old habits that lead to emotional turmoil, negative thinking, poor health, and the cynical belief that you're living in a competitive world where you must fight to get what you need. Soon, however, well-being will be a common state for you. You'll return to wholeliness more easily and more often, and you'll see it manifesting in your life. Wounds you never thought could be healed will get better on their own. Discord will give way to harmony, and struggle will make way for acceptance and peace.

Adopting a lifestyle of wholeliness is comparable to adopting the habit of eating well. Let's say you're used to subsisting solely on poor-quality, processed foods. When you switch over to meals that include more fruits and vegetables, for example, you'll naturally experience an initial period of craving your old favorites. But this feeling passes quickly as you realize that by eating better, you're losing weight, gaining strength and energy, and improving your health. Soon, you no longer have the desire to consume junk. Similarly, applying wholeliness to your life may take some effort and self-control at first. But once you witness the wave of positive change that it brings you, you won't want to revert to your old, harmful ways . . . and you'll wonder how you ever lived any differently!

Cynicism, pessimism, and greed can be found everywhere, and it seems as if there are plenty of people out to hurt or take advantage of you. I know that it might not be easy to believe in the possibility of wholeliness or commit to manifesting it in this world. But if you repeatedly choose to do so, the distrust will begin to fade. Hold on to the beautiful feeling of connection whenever you experience it. Sense it in every fiber of your being at every opportunity. Delight in it, and say a prayer of gratitude for it. This is how you're meant to feel! Trust in the power of wholeliness, and you'll see that it provides not only hope, but real results. It will keep you going on your worst days.

I encourage you to set aside time each day to observe, pray, and act. At night, you might write down in a journal what you did that day to embrace wholeliness—and then take a few minutes to imagine, love, and pray a little more. Plan what you might do tomorrow to further foster wholeliness in your life and the lives of others. The possibilities are endless, but the accountability of checking in with yourself will help discipline you to begin living in this new way. You can also create accountability by surrounding yourself with supportive people who lovingly encourage you to embrace wholeliness instead of fear. (Note that you can meet like-minded individuals who believe in wholeliness by going to my Facebook page titled **Carmen Harra: Wholeliness.**)

Sacred Connections to Spirit and Each Other

Wholeliness is the all-important element that will allow us to survive the great challenges of this era in human history. To do so, we'll have to work cooperatively, even with those who have challenging behaviors and attitudes. We must be willing to get hurt or experience loss in order to come together with others.

As a global community, we will have to ensure that all of our most basic needs are met—from food, clothing, shelter, and safety, to freedom and happiness. We've been told so often not to trust our fellow human beings that we've often missed out on the support that others can give us. This is especially true in the West, I find. My perspective on this is very much colored by my having grown up in a Communist country where food was scarce—looking out only for oneself or one's own family was extremely unusual. There were so many of us who lacked the basics that it simply wouldn't have worked if everyone had behaved in this way. I counsel people from all over the world, and the experience of growing up in an "Old World" country has given me some insights into creating a supportive community (which I will share in the last part of this book).

As you seek to embody and project wholeliness, you'll find that you're relying more on the assistance of other people, as well as your cosmic, sacred connections to Spirit and those who have passed on. Like everyone, you need Divine intervention, and you can make that happen. You can feel fear as you think about the problems in the world—such as crumbling institutions and systems or disturbing global events—or you can take comfort in the fact that you aren't alone in your desire to heal the suffering that plagues humanity. By mending your heart, changing your thoughts and behaviors, and working to manifest wholeliness in your own life, you're going to make a difference . . . and you are *not* the only one who will do so.

Humanity is awakening to a higher level of consciousness; and more and more men, women, and children are loving and supporting each other. In the darkest corners of the earth, where there is the greatest amount of suffering, people are saying, "It's time to change!" They're opening their minds and hearts and rediscovering this sacred wisdom.

You're participating in this great change, too, even though you may not realize it. The fact that you picked up this book is a sure sign that you're embracing your power. Maybe you were drawn to it because you wanted to help yourself by opening to new ideas and getting back in touch with your heart and soul. I'm happy you made that choice. But you can go beyond this limited goal and actually help the entire human race!

I know it may seem hard to believe that you—as one person in a great big world of nearly seven billion people—have the ability to bring about wholeliness, but you're about to find your hope and courage rekindled.

With love, I ask you to join me in learning about and embracing this extraordinary gift of wholeliness.

PART I

A TIME FOR HEALING

GIVING BIRTH
TO A NEW
HUMAN EXPERIENCE

"When we are no longer able to change a situation . . .
we are challenged to change ourselves."

— **VIKTOR FRANKL**

Many people are gripped by the fear of a doomsday wiping out humankind. Yet the prophecies that have been made throughout history are projections of our fear onto a point of *change,* not a point of destruction. Our wild imaginations tend to lead us to misinterpret such warnings as indicative of a coming apocalypse. But we don't have to live as if we're on the brink of some sort of catastrophe. There's no need to adopt the attitude of *I'd better look out for myself because no one else will.* Rather, the old beliefs about competing with each other for survival are being replaced by a trust in cooperation as we give birth to a new human experience that's marked by the awareness that we are one. Blessed by sacred connections that offer us more hope for tomorrow, humanity will change for the better.

All of us long for both the power to improve our lives and the peace to accept what we don't have control over, but we're afraid that we can't have either. We think that we're powerless to transform our circumstances and eradicate the hardships that have plagued humanity throughout the ages. We even falsely believe that our God-given destiny is to suffer, or that peace can only exist in a perfect world with the absence of evil or destructive forces.

Our faith in the power of peace disappears the moment a cloud rolls in, because we've been taught that the only way to achieve harmony is to be ready at any moment to battle those who threaten us. Thanks to this mentality, we've become combative creatures and lost our innate sense of tranquility and cooperation. We're like dogs who bare our teeth menacingly the second another dog comes too close to their food. We are so wrong!

If we believe in, embrace, and work to manifest wholeliness, we'll experience strength, power, and contentment, and the old misconceptions will melt away. Our species will evolve in the way the ancient prophets foretold. We'll enter a new age of human experience and end a 26,000-year cycle, just as the wise Mayan elders predicted.

The Rebirth of Humanity

It's exciting to know that humankind is entering an entirely new era on Earth. Understandably, it's a little scary as well—we're not sure how we're supposed to adapt to the changes we're undergoing. We want our lives and the world to calm down and settle into predictability because that's what makes us feel safe. However, that's not going to happen in the immediate future. There are more transformations to come, more turbulence and uncertainty. This is inevitable.

Fortunately, you can learn to manage your response of stress and anxiety to the events of your life and what's happening around you, and take part in guiding humanity toward a better future that awaits. Only by joining forces with others can you diminish the fear and anxiety that accompany change. If you think that you have to manage this great shift and its uncertainty all on your own, you're buying into an illusion that contributes to your anxiety. Know that you are *not* alone.

You can learn to understand wholeliness and, as a result, be more aware of it working in your life. You can feel a sense of unity and interconnectedness with all. You're part of the whole and, at the same time, a sacred individual capable of healing yourself and bringing healing energy to those you meet. Heal yourself, and the world gets closer to a state of perfection.

Wholeliness is an idea that can never be completely achieved for an extended period of time in the material realm at this point in human history, but you can certainly believe in its force and strive to manifest it in yourself and your community. Just as you embrace justice, love, beauty, and compassion, you can embrace the remarkable surge of power and peace that wholeliness sends through your soul. Then you can begin to manifest wholeliness on Earth so that the people in your life and the situations you find yourself in are reflections of health, healing, and sacred unity with all creation.

● ● ●

Humanity is being reborn at this time—and just as with a real birth, it's only natural to feel frightened and confused. The intensity of the experience compels all of us to focus on what's going on right now. There's no way to continue to deny that we're in a time of great transition. Any woman who has delivered a baby can tell you that there are no distractions that could have taken her mind off what was happening with her body! These days, no amount of celebrity gossip, sunny forecasts from economic experts, or promises from politicians is enough to pull our attention away from the transformation all around us and the discomfort we're all feeling. And that's a good thing: we're finally paying attention to the situations that matter.

What's more, we've begun to look around us and see where help is coming from. Will we have assistance, guidance, and support? Will we find the strength and courage to see this birth process through to that magical moment when a new life emerges?

The answer is a resounding *yes!* We have all we need, right here at hand: the loving support, creativity, and power that will sustain, inspire, and encourage us.

To begin to feel this power, you must understand three truths about wholeliness:

1. Transformation begins within.

2. Momentum builds quickly as you unite with others.

3. Divine help comes when you need it most.

As long as you reject or overlook these truths—and humans have been doing so for quite some time—you will endure hardships. But if you embrace the three axioms of wholeliness, your life will become far easier and much less frightening. Keep in mind, though, that the work toward change will continue to be challenging on occasion; after all, labor pains are called that for a reason! For example, it's not fun to watch the economic crisis unfolding around the world and wonder how it will affect your job, your business, your savings, and those you care about. It's not easy to believe that in such a polarized world, human beings will find common ground and invent new systems and institutions that are much better than the ones we have now. Yet this is exactly what's happening already.

Technology has its dark side, but just as the bombs that were dropped on Hiroshima and Nagasaki awakened us to the potential to use atomic power for good or evil, all the suffering the world is currently experiencing is awakening us. And just as we have *not* destroyed our world despite having had the ability to do so with nuclear weapons for some time, we will not use technology to do further damage to ourselves. Instead, science will be key to our recognizing how interconnected we all are—we'll discover how personal healing and joy can spread to others in ways we could never have imagined just a few years ago. Be assured that the agitation and distress around the globe will soon give way to something wonderful: a new age of human experience that's dominated by a spirit of cooperation, not competition.

The Three Truths of Wholeliness

Now I'd like to closely examine these three truths of wholeliness, along with the evidence that your perceptions have been distorted in a negative way. Each truth shines a light that will help you begin to see and manifest wholeliness in the world.

Truth #1:
Transformation Begins Within

It's a struggle to make changes outside of ourselves, where we have no control, but it's far easier to do so from the inside out! Too often, we concern ourselves with fixing other people, and then feel frustrated by our lack of progress. We're going about this all wrong. Transformation begins within, and only when we alter our thoughts, feelings, and awareness.

A significant shift requires you to trust that the future can be even better than the past. You can't simply put Band-Aids on situations that are broken or worn-out. Major transformation—whether it's becoming a parent, leaving a relationship, starting a new career, or moving to a different city—can be terrifying. Yet if you can reconstruct your inner beliefs about yourself and how your life can be, the external work you need to do doesn't seem so overwhelming. If you are able to see all the support that's available—the opportunities you have to connect with others all around the world who would jump at the chance to help—you can take the first crucial step toward transformation.

Not long ago, I counseled a lovely young woman from my home country who told me that her dream was to become an actress, but no one in her small town, including her family, encouraged her. She told me that she'd found no acting classes or potential roles for herself, and wondered if I saw her dream becoming a reality in the future. I told her that I did see her onstage and on-screen, but that she needed to be willing to make big changes and take some risks. I explained that, just like her, I'd lived in a small town in a faraway land and dreamed of becoming a performing artist.

I managed to do so, even though traveling abroad was all but impossible and there was no way to easily communicate with people around the world at the time. Now we have the Internet, social media, and freedom in Eastern Europe that seemed completely out of the question just a few decades ago. I pointed out that all of these are tools that could help her.

Soon afterward, the girl called me again to report she'd been so inspired by our session that she'd done some online research, found someone in London willing to help her acquire an inexpensive living situation, made the move, and successfully auditioned at a prestigious drama school.

Like my client discovered, life can really open up when we start believing in a better future and take even the smallest step toward creating it. Nowadays, how many life transformations begin with a question typed into a search engine or the click of a mouse? Every day, it becomes easier to reach out and find support, and the future promises even more marvelous ways of communicating with others via technology.

Why do people claim that they're lonely, no one cares about them, and no one will help them? These are distorted beliefs that keep them in a state of depression and pessimism. Unfortunately, depressed individuals can't make the effort to find support until they change those beliefs. Until then, they won't be able to take advantage of all the possibilities before them.

A lack of vision is affecting humanity as a whole. All over the world, so many of us are preserving old institutions and systems because we don't believe that we can come up with something better. Collectively, we need to stop trying to tinker with what is broken and instead take the time to envision better ways of operating. This internal shift in thoughts and beliefs can then give us the courage to start the process of change.

When you recognize your sacred connections to God and the entire universe, you realize that you have unlimited assistance in your mission to make your life better. With this sense of optimism, it becomes easier to envision a better future for everyone and experience wholeliness. As you begin to have a clearer picture of what needs to happen, you'll start to see the steps you need to take in order to make the dream a reality.

Perhaps you've been avoiding the changes you know you have to make—or avoiding the reality that your life is already very different and there is no going back to what it once was. Resentment, nostalgia, anger, or sadness that your life took an unexpected and unwanted turn will attract to you people and circumstances that reflect these feelings. When you let go of the past and accept that you're exactly where you are right now, you can begin an inner reformation and imagine what could be.

• • •

Your internal thoughts and feelings truly are key not just to your own transformation but to the evolution of all humankind. Because your consciousness is part of a universal consciousness, your thoughts and emotions actually influence other people's, even when you're silent and don't think anyone knows what's going on inside of you.

Thoughts can now be observed in the realm of the physical senses: When a thought occurs, neural networks and synapses become active. This activity can be observed using instruments such as a functional MRI (magnetic resonance imaging) machine. Researchers can actually "read" your thoughts to some degree by looking at a scan and seeing which areas of the brain "light up" on a screen displaying bioelectrical activity. These thoughts are also part of the collective consciousness, which is like an electrical grid (or, as I described earlier, a fabric of reality that operates separately from our five senses). And thanks to the law of nonlocality—one of the Eleven Eternal Principles from my book by the same name—one "corner" of the fabric can communicate instantaneously with another corner and affect its very nature.

Your thoughts don't exist in isolation in your brain. That's why inner transformation of thoughts and emotions (which also have a biological reality in the form of neuropeptides) influences others. From now on, you must never believe that what's in your mind is confined only to your mind.

Just for a moment, instead of thinking about this book, focus on something that you find amusing. Let yourself smile or laugh. As you do so, you're changing the activity in your brain, in your small corner of the fabric of reality. And there's an immediate physical response: your body releases "feel good" hormones such as endorphins, your facial expression changes as your muscles respond to your emotions, and your other muscles release their tension.

While you may be aware of these connections between your mind and your body, don't forget that *all* human thoughts and feelings affect the physical world that consciousness created. For instance, if you smile at a friend, that can cause him to smile, too. Or if you laughed really hard at the "reality" you created in your mind just a second ago, someone else in the room may have chuckled and then wondered aloud, "What's so funny? Do share!" You actually influenced that person's behavior, and with very little effort. This is an example of how thoughts, emotions, and consciousness affect the external world locally by altering the frequency of energy in that area. The more intuitive you are, the more easily you'll pick up on the shifts created when other people change their own thoughts or emotions.

The effect of one person's internal changes can be nonlocal as well. Your laughing may cause someone thousands of miles away to laugh as well, or to notice her mood suddenly becoming much more positive. If this sounds far-fetched, keep in mind that this is a scientific truth. In quantum physics, it's known as "the butterfly effect": it's said that the beating of a butterfly's wings can cause a storm halfway around the globe because of an interconnectedness at the smallest level of reality (subatomic particles and waves).

If you pay close attention, you can observe your effect on other people or your own body. For this reason, it's important to remember that your thoughts, just like any other part of you, require at least some degree of discipline to ensure that they're positive.

Should you alter your thoughts to be closer in alignment to wholeliness, you'll find that you feel a sense of expansiveness, hope, and possibility regardless of what's happening in your life. Optimism will arise, inspiration will awaken, and you'll open the channels that allow your mind to recognize messages from Spirit. The Divine will flood your heart and mind with love, abundance, wisdom, and ideas. You'll be filled with the light of illumination— of peace, joy, creativity, hope, faith, beauty, and guidance.

The mind is so used to falling into old habits that you may grow impatient and start thinking, *I don't trust that this will work. Divine guidance isn't there for me.* Yet it always is, and with time and continuity, you will begin to feel it.

The transformation begins with you. It begins *inside of* you.

Truth #2:
Momentum Builds Quickly as You Unite with Others

When people are united by similar ambitions and come together with the intention of helping to heal the world, they can accumulate the force of an unstoppable hurricane. The energy of the universe enters their bodies, minds, and souls and endows them with the power to produce constructive change. Individuals find themselves encouraging each other and employing their own strengths to compensate for the weaknesses of those around them. Each person adds one more source of willing energy, and this continues until there's enough to actually transform the world.

There's a reason the Divine blessed individuals with a few specific talents: if we're each good at something, then together we're good at everything! Working together in a spirit of wholeliness and cooperation, every one of us experiences being a piece that composes and serves the complete whole. Divinely inspired momentum builds quickly because we're united, drawing upon everyone's talents.

Having said all that, while progress will come at the appropriate time, at this moment humanity is in a season of change, and this process must inevitably start with some discomfort. Therefore, you may feel pessimistic during this stage and wonder what you can possibly do to make a difference in this troubled world. Maybe you work with others for a common cause and feel dispirited at times when, despite your efforts to defuse the situation, the group gets bogged down in petty disagreements. You might be a very positive and giving person, yet you find that some people don't respond when you act kinder, more lighthearted, or more compassionate. This is not because you're failing to make a difference, I promise you.

Many individuals are simply overwhelmed by their feelings of fear, anger, and sadness. They look around and see greed and selfishness and start to believe that they have to be tough or even cruel to protect themselves. They worry that others can't be trusted to do their jobs, and as a result, they become more controlling.

People who are fearful can develop a hard shell that doesn't let anything in very easily. If you encounter these individuals often, you might start to wonder if you're the only one who is hopeful and cheerful. You may even start to think that you're a little crazy for not buying into the doubts and cynicism of others. You're not!

Additionally, I'm sure that there are days when you turn on the television and it seems as if humankind is further away than ever from achieving a harmonious, healthy, and functional society. (Who doesn't feel this way?) Or you might feel worn down by the squabbles between family members, neighbors, and others who seem bent on creating conflict. But if you keep working on transforming yourself on the inside, others will recognize how peaceful you are and be inspired to adopt your habits. If you slip into pessimism, remember that you can't see everything that's happening in the world or inside people's minds. Your patience and compassion might be affecting people more profoundly than you imagined.

The human species is nearly at the tipping point, and a huge shift in global consciousness is inevitably approaching. Whatever you're doing to create a sense of inner peace and joy, continue to do so and have faith in its power. Whatever you're doing to effect positive change in your family, your workplace, and the larger community, keep it up and don't get discouraged. Your efforts, and those of like-minded individuals, will very soon pay off in a monumental way.

If you're skeptical, think back to the biggest shifts you've experienced in your own life. Pressure built . . . and then, seemingly from out of nowhere, dramatic change occurred, didn't it? Often when a big moment finally comes, it spreads at the speed of light. Have patience and faith.

• • •

The amount of time it takes to get to the point of great transformation can be frustratingly long. Even so, after the pivotal event, we tend to forget how agonizing the wait was and the difficulties of the struggle. Standing on the other side of history, we don't imagine what it must have been like to have wondered if we would ever see the changes that seemed as if they'd never come about.

I'm reminded of when Secretary of State Hillary Clinton was a senator from New York running for President of the United States, and her mother was with her on the campaign trail. In a speech, Senator Clinton noted that when her mother was born, women in America couldn't even vote, but now she could vote for her own daughter to be President. This monumental change, which was a long time in the making, came about very quickly when the tides shifted. In fact, it's now something that we take for granted . . . so much so that we've already forgotten how impossible it once seemed. That's the nature of how we experience great transformations: they take forever, we start to lose hope, they happen, and then we forget how long and difficult the struggle was. But the important thing to remember is that they always do occur.

When a change is in the works, you can't always see its effects. That's because, as I've previously said, it begins on the inside when people start to think and perceive differently. It's impossible to peer inside their heads and know that they're preparing for a shift. Very often, they're simply waiting for the moment when someone else makes the first move. Then an army of supporters is suddenly behind that first person, willing to step out or speak up.

How many people does it take before the effect is great enough to cause the larger whole to embrace courageous transformation? A quote that has often been attributed to anthropologist Margaret Mead says: "Never doubt that a small group of thoughtful, committed citizens can change the world." I would add that we should never doubt that a small group of those who hold compassion and love in their hearts can change humanity. In fact, we're about to see that happen.

Truth #3:
Divine Help Comes When You Need It Most

Whenever you feel troubled, the Divine will shower mercy upon you and come to the rescue. You have a powerful, sacred connection with God. It's essential to remember that someone out there loves you and will always be there for you: the Divine Force, which works via people. God will send you someone to remind you that you are loved. Granted, it can be very difficult to make yourself believe this in your lowest moments, but it's true. . . .

Throughout history, a person who is suffering has often been depicted as falling to her knees, spreading her arms open, and casting her eyes upward to the heavens. This kneeling figure has become a universal representation of prayer to the Divine. Similarly, the ancient Egyptians who worshipped Ra, the sun god, faced the sun to drink in its vitalizing power. And the Hindus' yogic position of the sun salute, often performed at sunrise, was their way of appealing to their sun god, Surya.

Why does it come so naturally to us to look toward the heavens for help? We humans instinctively feel the force of the Divine radiating down upon us from the sky; we sense something is out there beyond our planet that's loving, merciful, and powerful enough to help us transcend the suffering we experience. Intuitively, the ancients recognized that the sun is responsible for bringing life to Earth. Today, science says that they were right, because lifeforms can't exist without the sun's energy. Consequently, we direct our gaze up and beyond our planet as we ask for help to extinguish our pain.

That which is above us is transcendent and less heavy than we are. We sense that our burdens will fall away if the light from the sky can infuse us and bring us relief. We instinctively know that our toxic beliefs, thoughts, and feelings weigh us down. Instead, we should be lifted up and transported to a place where we can look down at our troubles from the perspective of a bird surveying the land below. We long to soar, and the invigorating warmth of the sun gives us hope that darkness and storms will move away. We absorb the light knowing that it offers a positive resolution to our problems. After all, people who aren't exposed to enough sunlight develop a variety of ailments, including depression. We're absolutely meant to soak in the light.

We all require Divine help right now so that we may overcome the problems we've created for ourselves and begin to envision what we'll discover next. We need to see the potential that lies beyond the next mountain, which feels like an impenetrable obstacle when we're earthbound. We're facing the ruin *and* rebirth of our world as we know it, and this scares us. Yet just as the early humans who looked to the sky for power and blessings, we sense that the forces from above can help us emerge safely from these monumental changes—some of which are looming in the near future, and many that have already begun.

Across the world, the Divine Force is working through us to help those who desperately require aid. Volunteers, organizations, churches, charities, governments, and individuals do the sacred work of healing. Sponsoring a poor child, adopting a homeless animal, or assisting disadvantaged individuals in our communities —these are all ways in which the Divine is using us to give support to those in great need.

Take, for example, Vital Voices, which was founded in 1997 by Hillary Rodham Clinton and is an organization I'm involved with. Vital Voices helps women in the most dire situations all around the world: those who are in danger of being tortured or killed for trying to achieve an education, earn money to feed their families, or free themselves from an arranged marriage or abusive spouse.

Many celebrities are involved with Vital Voices and try to bring attention to this worthy cause. Each member finds a way to make a difference using his or her specific talents and connections— I am active on the benefits committee, for instance, and have designed the medal that represents the organization. Whenever I do anything with them, I feel part of a large and sacred force of people who are trying to help strangers simply because it's the right thing to do.

Every time I attend a Vital Voices meeting, I come out of it with a buzzing sensation that I know is the energy of love and enthusiasm. I truly believe that every person can have this experience by joining up with others to contribute to the planet in a positive way, whether it's providing relief for sea animals harmed by oil spills or pets that have been mistreated or abandoned.

• • •

Human beings are like plants in that we take the light and transform it into nourishment, only our light is love itself. We need only to turn our faces to the sun, to the powerful force of a loving Spirit who wants us to be revitalized, and remind ourselves of the love that can pour into our hearts. Just like tiny blades of grass pushing through a crack in the sidewalk and stretching toward the sky, we can receive Divine light even when our circumstances seem to confine us. Nature breaks through asphalt and stone, reclaims ancient pyramids, and continually stretches toward the source of its power . . . while whispering to us that we should do the same. What's been broken can often be repaired simply by the power of love moving people to do healing work. Whatever has been lost can be replaced.

To that end, one of my favorite Bible stories is that of Job, who lost all that he had and yet would not give up his love for God. The first thing Job did upon discovering his horrific loss was to instinctively fall to the ground and bless God rather than curse him for bringing a flood of change into his life. Ultimately, this hero ended up with great abundance: more children, wealth, and joy than ever before. Like Job, we may find that after a loss we go on to experience something even better that perhaps we never envisioned.

I understand how grief from a loss can lock you into thoughts about the past and blind you to the opportunities for a better future. It's hard to be optimistic when you're full of sorrow. Yet if you look to Spirit for support and help, you can begin to imagine that the sun will shine upon you again.

Many religious traditions have stories about great floods that God sent to sweep away crops, people, and animals—from Noah's ark to *The Epic of Gilgamesh.* In reality, the sediment left behind by a river that has flooded may be just what the soil needs to be replenished with nutrients that foster new growth. What may feel like Divine retribution is actually a necessary clearing away of the old so that something new can be brought in. Spirit doesn't want to hurt or punish anyone, but if we insist on living on a flood-plain, we're not working in sync with Divine Forces. We're acting as if we live in isolation from, or opposition to, the planet. Living cooperatively and sustainably on the earth requires us to respect its rhythms, and one of these rhythms is the weather. It means accepting that change is part of life and resistance only leads to suffering. We have to work *with* the Divine flow of energy, not against it.

Metaphorically speaking, we've built modern civilization on a floodplain, and we must tolerate our systems being swept away in order to clear the way for what's next: systems that are more in tune with Divine ideals such as wholeliness. Spirit never in-tended for us to create structures that divide people as our cur-rent economic, government, social, and religious institutions do. The intense and completely unexpected floods, earthquakes, hur-ricanes, and tsunamis we're experiencing as a result of global cli-mate change are reminders that we're meant to live in harmony with each other and the planet. They're meant to wake us up so that we begin to work with Spirit to devise better ways of organiz-ing ourselves and our communities. Natural disasters mirror the disaster of our unbalanced lifestyles. Help is coming, but first we need to clear away what we don't need—and we'll have Divine aid to assist us with that task.

Divine assistance doesn't always feel helpful, since it challeng-es us to resolve our inner issues and cease creating more suffering for ourselves and others. Change may seem destructive to us, but later we're often able to see the good that came from a transfor-mation we resisted. With hindsight, we can see our own role in working against Spirit, who had our best interests in mind. We should never blame God for that which we've had a hand in creating, as He urges us to experience wholeliness; perceive the unity of all things; envision a world in which all people have shelter, safety, and freedom; and work toward a human race that lives in a sustainable way.

Divine help is not separate from our actions; in fact, it drives them. Our job is to connect to this force, let it fill us with passion, and then allow it to direct us. We are beautiful instruments of our Divine Creator, and we should allow ourselves to be moved by God's hand as if we're pieces on a chessboard. If we play our part and find the strength, creativity, and compassion we didn't know we had, we can eradicate our feelings of fear and disconnection—we can start to believe again in the power of wholeliness.

Soon, abundance will appear before our eyes, and we'll realize that it's only a manifestation of the abundance that was there all along—we'd simply overlooked it. We have no idea just how great our potential is for creation and evolution!

How to Embrace the Three Truths of Wholeliness and Participate in the Birth of a New Human Experience

Observe

Make a choice to stop yourself the next time you feel angry or judgmental and ask: "Is there any way in which I exhibit the same behavior that's upsetting me?" Even if you only show it in a minor way, make a mental note of this.

Think about how the human race is changing for the better. In fact, you might want to keep a list documenting the ways in which people all around you are striving to bring about wholeliness and turn away from self-centeredness and greed. Include yourself, your friends, your neighbors, your family members, and even strangers. Be sure to review the list often, for it will contradict the common notion that everyone is out for him- or herself, which is a destructive and pervasive belief. So whenever you see that you're holding on to it, let it go!

Pray

No matter what happens in your life, ask the Divine to show you what you must do to come out of any situation well.

Say a prayer that you may transform your fear into love and courage, and that you may better exemplify the ideal of wholeliness. Try: *Help me be the change I'd like see in the world.* Whatever you see as a problem, pray to be a channel for the solution. For example: *Help me embody justice and be just in my thoughts and my actions. Help me be peaceful and express peace with my words and in my behavior. Help me be respectful of my body and the physical world around me.* Spirit will assist you in being all that you desire to be.

Pray that you might see evidence that change is happening, that you aren't alone in your yearning for equality, unity, harmony, and an end to suffering. Thank the Divine for the momentum that's already shifting human consciousness toward wholeliness—and, as you do, feel yourself participating in this enormous transformation.

Rather than being angry at the leaders in your government or your community, pray that they will feel the Divine presence in their lives and turn toward wholeliness and love. As you feel Spirit fill you with compassion that revitalizes you, send this powerful light toward those who still cling to the old, destructive, divisive ways. Pray for terrorists, that they may be awakened and enlightened; and pray for yourself, that you may find the strength to heal the part of you that's angry and leans toward being cruel and domineering. Ask for the strength of love to infuse you.

• • •

One way to pray effectively is to go out in nature and situate yourself so that you have a clear view of the heavens. Meditate on your dilemma, pray for the Divine to show you how to reach a resolution, and then study the sky. Absorb its endless grace. Notice clouds gliding lazily by, hundreds of raindrops plunging to the ground, or the moon silently commanding the oceans' water levels to rise and recede. This method of communicating with Spirit is extremely important. Don't become so busy that you're rushing around trying to complete all the tasks you think you must. Make it a priority to sit and behold the Divine creation that is nature and the heavens.

As you watch the sky, open up about your troubles and ask Spirit to send you peace so that your burdens no longer weigh you down. After a few minutes of this prayer technique, you'll feel more at ease about whatever you're going through. Later on in the day or week, you might notice hints of a resolution to your dilemma. If someone you love has passed away, perhaps you feel his reassuring presence—even a sense that he's helping, nurturing, and supporting you in the same way he did when he was with you on Earth. If you've lost your job, maybe you'll receive a phone call about another opportunity or run into an unexpected HELP WANTED sign. Or if you have health concerns, you might notice them improve within the next few days after performing this exercise. Be open to how your requests to God get answered. Prayer is a powerful action; don't overlook the evidence of its effectiveness.

This technique of sky gazing and contemplation calms us during hard times and connects us to the invisible forces beyond our reach so that we may find the impetus to change our actions.

Act

Throughout this book, I'll suggest specific actions that will help you believe in, and achieve, wholeness in your life. To begin, start a journal where you can write down your thoughts as you work through the tasks at the end of each chapter. Also create a to-do list separate from your journal, where you'll record the specific actions you're going to take. When you make your list, leave a space next to each item so you can jot down the date you actually did it. Some of the actions I suggest may seem too challenging right now, but write them down anyway and schedule a date for completion on your calendar. Don't just think about how all of this sounds very lovely. Observe. Pray. Act.

Use your journal in combination with your to-do list and calendar to hold yourself accountable for inner transformation. Change for the better begins within; it begins with you!

The new human experience can't come into being unless enough people choose to participate in the birthing process and consciously create wholeness to where it begins to manifest. However strong our feelings of despair and powerlessness are, there's a cure for them: wholeness. Remember that turbulence offers a grand opportunity for transformation. The Divine Force is supporting you in adopting a new consciousness. Let go of your mind's resistance to this idea and explore the possibilities of what you can do to help the world!

In the next chapter, you'll learn just how important it is to release your fears and embrace a sense of possibility. No matter what challenges you face, you must have faith that you can make your life better. Eradicating fear is crucial.

·· ● ··

CHAPTER
2

TURN FROM FEAR TO POSSIBILITY

"What is needed, rather than running away or controlling or suppressing or any other resistance, is understanding fear; that means, watch it, learn about it, come directly into contact with it. We are to learn about fear, not how to escape from it..."

— JIDDU KRISHNAMURTI

All of humanity is in a time of great uncertainty and change. Even if your own life is relatively stable, it's natural to feel that you aren't secure, that a great tide could sweep through and alter your experience. Many people have come to believe this thanks to an economic crisis that has rocked the world. Others have developed a sense of insecurity because they recognize that global warming is a very real threat. The 2010 oil spill in the Gulf of Mexico was a wake-up call for many, too, just as the 2001 terrorist attacks. How can we feel safe and believe in the future when there's mounting evidence that the whole world has gone mad?

Although going through a time of transformation and rebirth can be frightening and painful, change always offers a chance to create something even better to replace what's been lost, because it sweeps away harmful situations. You can actually let go of your apprehension, worry, and dread and become excited about the possibilities before you. Look closely at why you're scared and what you're scared of, and you'll see that your fear only has power because you've given it power. When you choose to stop letting fear rule your life and hold you back, you can joyfully and eagerly embrace the opportunity to make your life better and participate in the healing of human suffering.

Taking the Anxiety Out of Change

Globally, people sense that major changes are happening, and they're anxious to know where humanity is headed. Institutions we've believed in as far back as we can remember are extremely unstable, like towers built on faulty foundations. Banks and major corporations are collapsing. Nations are having to bail each other out because their finances are all interconnected. Individuals are losing their homes or waking up to the realization that they owe more money than their mortgages are worth. Young people are saddled with debt, and not just from school, housing, or credit cards—they're having to pay for their *countries'* deficits, too. The Catholic Church is reeling from scandals of priests molesting children, while other churches are in conflict about social issues such as gay marriage. Considering all of this turmoil, it's not hard to see why folks are increasingly unable to fall asleep at night or are suffering from bouts of depression and anxiety. It's true that problems surround us, but real solutions are not far away.

Like many, you may have turned to the regular use of mood-altering substances—whether it's alcohol, antidepressants, or any other drug—to cope with the chaos swirling inside you. While these remedies may work for a while, using them simply creates more problems. What's more, your subconscious mind is always aware of when you're scared and out of control. You may be thinking, *I'll be okay,* but deep inside there's a voice saying, *Are you crazy? Your life is a mess! Disaster is all around you!*

Even if you haven't turned to a source of chemical comfort, when you have an upsetting conversation with a family member who is constantly getting into trouble with his finances or even with the law, or you read in the news about a violent crime, the fear deep within you grows stronger. Yet your fear can also be increased by any evidence that your world is changing—situations that at one point seemed rock solid may suddenly feel as if they're washing away.

When we look at the economic problems all over the world, we can't help but worry about our own financial security, and rightly so, since we're all interconnected and none of us individually has the power to fix the massive institutions that are failing. Related to this, many Americans are apprehensive about the revisions that have been made to health care and don't realize that the old system was already broken. (In reality, a new one was virtually unavoidable, and we've been putting off doing something about it for decades.)

The proper response to big changes that we can't control is to learn as much as possible about the topic, engage in dialogue with our fellow citizens, plan for how we'll adjust, and be prepared for both good outcomes and new problems that we'll need to address. Unfortunately, the most common thing to do is react with fear, sadness, or anger. These are all grief responses. We don't like letting go of the illusion that "Everything was fine just as it was" and "We didn't have to undergo a change." Yet the fact is, life changes. People change.

This fearful reaction to the falling away of the old and ushering in of the new occurs even when big things are happening all around you that are actually positive. When everyone you know is giving up poor eating habits and exercising more, are you happy for them and inspired to do the same? Or do you start feeling guilty and fearful, telling yourself: *I could never give up my sweets and my pasta. I can't stand exercise. I know I could never stick with that.* You might even admit some deeper concerns to yourself: *Now that my friends are getting together to exercise, I feel left out, because I don't want to do that.*

The subconscious mind is skilled at creating pessimistic thoughts. That's why it's common to respond to change with resistance and negativity instead of automatically seeing the possibility that doing something different could turn out to be positive.

Wake-Up Calls

Today, all of us realize that we must make alterations in our lives due to circumstances beyond our control. As I mentioned, the disastrous oil spill in the Gulf of Mexico was a wake-up call for many. It was the result of an illusion of disconnection, and reflected our unwillingness to embrace wholeliness. People put their own needs and desires ahead of everyone's health and well-being. From the executives at BP (formerly British Petroleum) who shrugged off environmental rules and safety procedures, to the government officials who looked the other way and the consumers who refused to take responsibility for their insatiable need for oil, many individuals played a part in this disaster of our own making. Ultimately, this catastrophe, like most others, stemmed from too many overinflated egos. Yet each of us can prevent similar crises in the future by accepting that we must find alternatives to fossil fuels, and by supporting each other in developing green energy and conserving gasoline and oil.

Humankind has been blessed with an abundant planet that renews itself, cleanses itself, and provides for us again and again. Unfortunately, we're not acting as good stewards of our planet and respecting what's been given to us. We're constantly wanting more than we need and hoarding what we have instead of sharing it and being frugal. The earth cannot continue to produce as much as we're demanding and is beginning to show signs of collapse. Fortunately, this era of insatiability and gluttony is coming to an end. It has to, since we can't continue at this pace of consumption and selfishness.

On a grander scale, the budget deficits of countries around the world, which so many of us are worried about, reflect a way of operating that isn't working anymore. People everywhere have been acting from the fear that they won't be able to have the lifestyle they desire—by borrowing too much from the next generation, taking too much from the earth, and making poor choices. Much of what was "borrowed" was wasted, and now individuals are having a hard time paying back what they've been lent. All of these situations are reversible, but only if we admit to what we've done and agree to make better choices. Sometimes we have to invest in the future vision, but when we're using valuable resources to build up temporary wealth, that's not responsible—and that's what we've been doing.

Some of us have woken up to the challenges that face us; after all, the severe weather patterns and seismic events that we've been experiencing are impossible to ignore. Nature is rebelling against us because we've chosen to rebel against it for so long. Mother Earth is responding to our assaults with angry outbursts, releasing her frustration through floods, earthquakes, and hurricanes that are growing in power. In December 2009, I predicted that 2010 would be the year of earthquakes; within just a few months, we'd experienced huge ones in Chile and Haiti, as well as other areas around the world.

Global climate change and tectonic activity are the scientific reasons for most of these unusually severe catastrophic events, but another way to explain what's going on is that we've upset the balance of the planet, which is responding with intensity. Because we're part of Spirit, it's fair to say that we, as part of Divine consciousness, are giving ourselves our own wake-up call. We're being roused out of our deep slumber so that we'll answer the call of transformation and seize it as an opportunity to evolve.

From Denial and Blame to Acknowledgment and Responsibility

When it comes to those who have behaved irresponsibly, I don't want to spend my time criticizing them. Instead, I want to stress that so many of us have gotten caught up in trying to figure out who is to blame for our broken systems, when what we should be doing is simply accepting that they're broken and that every one of us has to do his or her part to create better solutions. Some of us may have lived very conscientiously and resent having to deal with the consequences of the choices that we didn't personally make . . . but that attitude gets us nowhere. Being angry at those who were the most greedy or disrespectful is understandable, but that anger is toxic and has to be rejected.

It's not always easy to shift out of anger, resentment, or blame. And when we feel that we've done everything right, we may begrudge having to clean up what so often seems to be "someone else's mess"! Difficult though it may be to accept, we'll always have to deal with problems we didn't personally create but are affecting us nevertheless. We'll always face changes that aren't entirely of our own making, but giving in to fear and a sense of futility is very self-destructive.

We don't like to look at our roles in problems, or to accept that our ability to control the amount and timing of changes in our lives is limited. Our real power is in controlling our thoughts and perceptions. This is what allows us to accept what we can't have much of an impact on, such as national economic crises; we can then change what we can, such as discovering new ways of earning and managing money and creating security for the future.

This brings to mind my client Carrie, who lost a lot of money in her 401(k), only to regain it when the stock market climbed back upward again. The money may have been recovered, but her fear of not having enough to fund her retirement became very powerful, which made her realize that she hadn't made much progress in saving for the future in the last decade. Instead of taking responsibility for what she could do about her situation, Carrie railed against the bankers and financiers who had sent her and so many people on an unwanted roller-coaster ride. And the fact that she had friends who were in the very same situation wasn't giving her any comfort. Desperate to know what the future held for her financially, she gave me a call.

Now, Carrie is self-employed and quite successful. She's smart about her investments, and I'm sure she'll do well in the future. But in dealing with this stressful situation, a different problem had arisen: she hadn't been paying attention to her health. It's important to understand that security is not just about having money—that's a very limited way to look at it. Because I look at the whole picture when I do a counseling session, I suggested that she needed to address her physical issues by doing much more than relying on medication to treat her symptoms, as she had been. I urged her to adopt a healthier lifestyle.

Looking into Carrie's future, I did see financial security, but the ability to enjoy her retirement would be very brief due to medical issues. I told Carrie that she had the power to change this probable future, but only if she was willing to let go of her fears about money and face her real challenge: returning her body to a healthier state. She would have to let go of blaming others for her sense of insecurity and create a better future for herself by attending to herself as a whole.

In times of transformation, we long for certainty. When giving birth, we just want the baby to be born and the pain and uncertainty to end. However, like giving birth, transformation is a process. In the process of human evolution, which we're currently experiencing, we're all at the point of having to accept that there's no turning back and no avoiding the discomfort. After all, labor isn't going to stop, and the baby isn't going to return to the womb!

Instead of panicking about the state of the world and your own security, you have to let go of the fear, blame, and denial that keep you feeling helpless to work with your changing circumstances. If you focus on others' faults, you'll overlook your own power. Accept your situation exactly as it is right now, and let go of the idea that you can't change it for the better. You can!

From Fearful Resistance to Courageous Introspection

Resistance to change comes from fear. We like the certainty of knowing what's going to happen next, and we're comforted by the familiar. This is why we try to ignore the depth of our problems and tell ourselves that we need only to make a few small alterations here and there.

Returning to the example of the massive oil spill in the Gulf of Mexico, it was obvious that many of us didn't want to look below the surface—literally and figuratively—when it first occurred, because that might require us to consider our dependence on fossil fuels and deep-ocean drilling. While there were those who merely skimmed the surface and said, "It doesn't look so bad," underneath the waves were plumes of oil that we now know have sunk to the ocean floor and created a huge dead zone. Just because we don't see something doesn't mean it isn't there! And yet too often, we think this way because making big changes scares us. What if we make a mistake? What if we can't figure out what to do? What if we make matters worse? Even if we don't feel that we're ready for the challenge, there's simply no way to avoid the difficulty of facing our fears.

You too may need to make big changes in your life. Denial and resistance feed your fear because there's no fooling the subconscious mind, which senses that there's no returning to your former situation—even when your conscious mind is saying otherwise. In time, you start to feel fatigued and depressed because denying the reality of change is exhausting.

When you're liberated from the constant effort to pretend that everything is okay, it's a huge relief. Problems will actually begin to seem less daunting because the simple act of facing them reminds you that you do have the power to control your thoughts. Once you turn them away from the illusion that you can return to the "good old days," you'll start to see that you can, in fact, handle the truth about your circumstances. Freed from the burden of denial, you'll feel a glimmer of hope that maybe you *can* handle this transformation after all.

This is exactly what happened to Alicia, who sought my counsel about her relationship with a man named Jonathan. She was head over heels in love with him, and wholeheartedly believed that she would marry him. For almost two years, she'd fantasized about their wedding. She constantly sent him e-mails and love letters, and even showed up at his house uninvited. Jonathan never reciprocated, but Alicia was in denial regarding his lack of feelings for her.

Alicia followed my advice to meet with Jonathan and ask him flat-out how he felt about her and if marriage was on his mind. He sat her down and told her politely but unyieldingly that he did not want to be with her . . . in fact, he was gay. Heartbroken, Alicia left the meeting in tears.

In a few days, however, she experienced an epiphany: she had been completely out of touch with reality because of her fear that she would never find someone to love her. As painful as this belief was, letting it rise to the surface gave her a deep sense of freedom and relief. The shock of realizing how deep her denial was, and how much stress and emotional pain she'd caused herself by clinging to a fantasy, woke her up. Alicia seriously began to consider what I'd been saying to her about improving her self-esteem and decided that she was ready to work on her feelings of low self-worth in therapy. Like so many people, she'd been listening to her ego's fear and clinging to denial—not realizing that in doing so, she was simply causing herself more pain.

After acknowledging your own challenges, you can begin to look at your fears and analyze their sources. Most fears are irrational and not warranted. Fears that *are* rational are useful because they wake you up to the situations and problems you need to address. You have to stop stoking their flames with anxious thoughts, however, for it will be much easier to begin conquering what scares you and opening up to your great power to transform and evolve.

From Powerlessness to Action Rooted in Wholeliness

Wholeliness is the natural state of the universe, but our choice as souls to create this world of our senses caused us to develop amnesia about our sacred connections to Spirit and all those individuals in the world who would support us in bringing about positive change. When we set aside our very human fears and remember these connections, our feelings of division and suspicion begin to fade.

There are many unscrupulous, egotistical, frightened people who are watering the seeds of conflict instead of fostering unity and working together. It isn't easy to remember wholeliness when we see so much corruption and greed around us, but it's important not to engage in finger-pointing or perceive ourselves as helpless victims, as we may be encouraged to do. All of us have responsibilities as well as the ability to alter our thinking and behavior. We can and must choose the path of positive action.

We have to identify and then banish our fears to access our creativity and envision a better world, one with new institutions and systems that are more reflective of wholeliness. Only then will it begin to manifest. Fear is no excuse for inaction!

Whenever I speak to people about the big changes we're facing and the fact that our current way of operating isn't sustainable, they tend to have one of two responses to my prognostications: (1) either they deny the scope of the problem; or (2) they become depressed and feel powerless, saying, "Humanity can't possibly evolve and save itself." Many individuals would rather be pessimists than face an uncertain future, because this attitude at least offers them a certain sense of comfort in believing that they know what tomorrow holds. The reality is that if we can embrace wholeliness, we'll find our courage and act boldly—we'll change our mind-set and behaviors so that our small corner of the whole can change. If we focus on how much power we don't have—how we can't personally make a difference—then we'll become depressed and give up. But if we focus on wholeliness, we'll see that every small act of healing does have an impact. And then we can imagine creating a better world.

We can make the future wonderful, or we can cause tremendous suffering. It's up to us. We're at a crossroads. Because all of us are connected, the more of us who are embracing and working toward wholeliness, the quicker our progress will be.

I know these are scary times. Getting in touch with your fears can make you uncomfortable, but discomfort is part of the process of transformation and evolution. When you acknowledge and examine what frightens you, you'll notice that these things are based in false ideas about your separateness from the whole. You'll also realize that many of your fears are not necessary; they may even be quite illogical. Wholeliness will help you see how foolish and destructive these beliefs are, and you'll start replacing them with healthier ones.

Wholeliness Conquers the Fear of the Unknown

By nature, we stick with tradition and custom. If we've always done things a certain way, we often try to continue with that method forever. Change is difficult because it generates a sense of insecurity and instability; yet paradoxically, we're attracted to, and allured by, the possibilities it may bring. We'd like to think that something better awaits us, but our deep-rooted fear says, "You're crazy! Life can't get better!"

We all must understand that we can believe in the future and our power if we let go of our fear. Wholeliness allows us to embrace the mystery of not knowing what the future holds or what solutions we'll discover, for it shows us that we're never alone or without assistance—we don't have to envision and create a better life for ourselves all on our own.

Growing up in a country where it was impossible to leave without the government's permission, my dream of coming to America was, on the surface, preposterous. I'm sure many of the people of my town were quite amused by my ambitious goals as a child, particularly my insistence that someday I'd be on television in the U.S. I might as well have announced that I was starting my own country on Mars! But even though I had no clue how I was going to get from where I was to where I wanted to go, I was able to believe in my dream because I had great faith in the Divine. I knew that God would support me and present me with opportunities and individuals who could help me. Because of my intuitive gifts, I knew that my visions were not foolish or crazy.

In my work, I encourage others to develop their own intuition and become more aware of the synchronicities and mysterious connections between events and encounters in their lives. I want them to experience the confidence that I had in my ability to perceive connections that others couldn't see. I ask my clients, "Do you see this?" or "Does this make sense to you? Do you agree?" because I want them to listen to what *their* intuition is telling them, along with mine.

I've told clients what I see down the road for them, and they've often scoffed because they're only listening to their rational mind and can't envision how they could end up in the situation I'm describing. Then they'll contact me years later to admit, "You won't believe this, but you were right!" What I see doesn't always come true, of course, since the future is just one of an endless number of possibilities (you'll learn more about this later). But when the "impossible" future they dream of actually comes to fruition, it can seem quite shocking.

Most of the time, people go through life falsely thinking that nothing will change all that much. Even when they've experienced monumental transformations in their daily lives, they buy into the old belief: *From now on, life will be pretty predictable.* Human minds work that way. That's why when dramatic shifts happen, most of us are very surprised and deeply discombobulated.

The way to become more comfortable with the unknown is to trust that whatever happens, Spirit—as well as all the spirits who surround you—is always looking out for your best interests. (Yes, you do have spirits surrounding you, which I'll talk more about later.) When you remember your connections to these Divine Forces and believe in the power of wholeliness, what you can't yet perceive will seem less scary.

The Divine will provide you with direction and, in time, show you what steps you need to take. Faith and courage will fill the spot in your heart formerly occupied by fear, and you can actually look forward to what's next and begin to get an inkling of what's ahead. Most important, you'll begin to realize that you were never meant to navigate through life and its problems by yourself: the Divine will be right there next to you through every up and down, like an ever-faithful friend.

Facing the Fear of Loss

One reason why you may fear and resist change is because you don't want to experience loss. If you look more closely at what you might have to give up, however, you just might realize that you can do without it after all.

For example, a friend of mine lived through a fire that destroyed many of her possessions. Although it was emotionally painful to lose some of these items, she realized it was in fact a relief that others were now gone. She'd felt obligated to hold on to furniture and personal items that belonged to her late parents, or that she meant to get around to using but never quite did. As she told me: "I realize that my mother is still connected to me and a part of my life even if I don't have her jewelry box, which she didn't particularly have any great love for anyway. I was just afraid to let go of what was once hers, even though she'd probably ask, 'Why are you hanging on to that old thing?'"

In a sense, all of us are clinging to things that are not serving us or giving us pleasure; rather, they're simply cluttering up our lives or weighing us down. These include beliefs we hold on to or systems that don't work for us anymore. Collectively, humanity needs to revisit many of the "things" it has held on to for a very long time and question whether they're truly needed. Do we need religions that divide us? Do we need complex financial structures and millions of jobs concerned only with fostering the illusion that genuine wealth is being created?

It may be difficult to imagine a totally different economic system, the end to divisive religious beliefs, or the demise of the prison system. But if we look back in history, we'll see that we've often experienced changes and losses that seemed incredible at the time, but which we soon accepted and began to take for granted. We lost the horse and buggy as our main mode of transportation, but we still get around. We lost the individual countries' currencies in most of Europe, yet this hasn't led to widespread economic disaster. Laws supporting racism in places like the United States are gone, but no one misses those.

The pace of change has been remarkable, but we haven't seen anything yet, as it is going to pick up and leave us all reeling. We can be afraid of this or we can feel exhilarated by the possibilities of finally fixing some of the problems that have plagued humankind for thousands of years.

These positive changes will occur as human beings start to let go of beliefs, emotions, and behavior patterns that aren't working anymore. But as I was reminded when I married my husband and became an American, with any change, even if it's good, there always comes a loss of some type.

Loss is difficult because we're creatures of habit, hardwired to hold on to the familiar rather than risk trying something new. We forget that when we open up and let the creativity of the Divine Source flow through us, we often come up with even better ideas. God created the universe. God and humans together created remarkable societies, art, and culture. Why wouldn't God be there to help each of us create something extraordinary?

It's hard to look forward when we're obsessed with the pain of loss or the fear of not being able to adjust to something new. Neurologists have found that when we're scared, the blood flow to the parts of the brain associated with optimism and creativity becomes severely limited because it's rushing to the areas associated with fear. Fear turns off our capacity to dream, imagine, and envision; it also prevents us from staying open to the Divine's ideas about what we might co-create by working with God, the ultimate, innovative, loving, and powerful Force.

Wholeliness eases our fears and reconnects us with our optimism and creativity because we know that the Divine Force is there for us, bringing us people and situations that will help us turn our dreams into reality. We don't have to solve all our problems by ourselves. We don't even have to know what the solution is . . . it will eventually come to us. After all, Spirit created a world of abundance. Be assured that help is always on the way!

To take advantage of that help, however, you have to do your part. You must loosen the grip of your ego, for that is the generator of all the fear that's holding you back and causing you not to trust in the sacred, healing connections that are always there for you. It's preventing you from changing on the inside, imagining the life you'd like, and taking action toward achieving your goals.

In the next chapter, you'll learn how your ego works so that you can better control it and not be a victim of its runaway, irrational fear.

How to Turn from Fear to Possibility

Observe

All of us are creatures of habit. We may dislike our habits, but we're reluctant to stray from them because we take a certain comfort in their familiarity.

Identify three habits of yours that are holding you back from creating better ones in your life or are no longer serving you. How did you develop them? Did they serve a purpose at the time? Are they harmful, and could you replace them with others that enhance your well-being?

Many of us are unaware that our habits may be creating anxious, negative, fearful thoughts. So the next time you feel anxious, stop yourself and ask, *What is my belief right now?* Examine that belief. Is it distorted and negative? Is it even true? Or is it a false idea that has roots in old fears about not being nurtured and cared for by the universe and the people in your life?

In addition, the next time you receive support from someone in any form, instead of brushing aside its significance, make a point of noticing it. Let yourself feel the positive energy that's arisen in you because of this assistance, no matter how small of an encouragement it may have been. Feel grateful, and express that gratitude. Then ask yourself, *How could I make a habit of observing the loving support that's provided to me? What would happen if I made a point of noticing when people are supporting me?*

You may want to explore the answers to these questions by writing in a journal. It can also be helpful to go back and look at how you've reacted to others' help in the past in order to be able to analyze the progress you're going to make toward letting go of fear and embracing wholeliness.

Pray

Every day, we hear about terrible losses that others experience. It can be overwhelming. It's to the point that within minutes of turning on the television, we see news of someone's tragedy. We don't realize it, but the constant barrage of bad news affects us—it generates fear, worry, and anxiety that are like toxins. This is because when we hear of others' suffering, we begin to assume that the same can or will happen to us, too.

To counteract any feelings of hopelessness, despair, or pessimism, pray for those who are enduring hardships. Make a list of people you wish to pray for every day. If your neighbor lost his job, for instance, or there's a student in your child's school who is undergoing chemotherapy, make a point of praying for those individuals daily. Ask that love, light, healing, and hope be brought into their lives. Ask for relief of their pain, and that they feel the strength of the Divine supporting them.

Pray for yourself as well. Request help in remaining hopeful and positive despite the losses or uncertainty in your life. Seek guidance and faith that everything will turn out in the end. Pray for reassurance, and you'll receive it.

As you pray for others and yourself, you'll begin to feel your sacred connections to all of humanity and the Divine. You'll remember your sacred connection to all of life and your power to bring joy, love, and healing to others. This will give you comfort and strength, making it easier to acknowledge your fears and begin to conquer them. You will also feel as if you've done a good deed just by praying for someone else: instead of sending out negative emotions, which is both detrimental to you and the other person, you have instead wished for him or her nothing but beautiful, healing energy.

Act

If you focus on your problems, you'll start to feel scared and powerless. Yet if you take positive action, no matter how small, those feelings will begin to fade quickly, and you'll start to feel optimistic. It's like the story of the starfish dying on the beach: A man was walking along the shore, tossing the creatures back into the sea, one by one, when another person came along and asked, "What's the point? There are thousands of starfish dying on the beach. What difference does it make to attempt to save them?"

The man replied, "It makes a difference to the starfish." It also makes a difference to the person saving them! In other words, doing something, *anything*, to make a situation better shifts you out of fear and powerlessness and into a sense of hope.

By doing for others, you'll recognize that while you may be the only one on the beach, you're actually not alone. As you begin the work, strangers who are passing by will stop and pitch in. One can turn into many very quickly, and the power of the whole will encourage you to keep going.

Find a way to help others that goes beyond spending a few seconds writing a check to a charity (although you should do that as well!). Identify something you worry about, a problem that causes you to feel fearful and pessimistic. What can you do today—before you go to bed tonight—to make a difference?

When you face your fears by tackling a problem in a small way, you'll start to feel the exuberance that's necessary to make a positive change. As you meet others who are already working on this problem, or ready to begin because they've been inspired by you, you'll feel even more excited and enthusiastic. The Divine will bring people and resources your way. This is the power of wholeliness at work.

> Start today. Find one thing, just one, that you can do today to make a difference. Then stop thinking about it and do it!

When it comes to the nature and role of the ego, the originator of our fears, keep in mind that we all have one. Egos are not all bad; actually, they're responsible for a very important function, as you'll see. And you may be surprised to discover that groups can share an ego as well! That brings us to the next chapter of this book, in which you'll learn how to balance your own ego and resist the tug of the group ego so that you can have power over your fears and begin to believe in wholeliness.

$$\cdot\cdot\ \bullet\ \cdot\cdot$$

CHAPTER
3

LOOSEN THE GRIP
OF YOUR EGO

"A human being is a part of the whole, called by us the 'Universe,'
a part limited in time and space. He experiences himself,
his thoughts and feelings as something separate from the rest—
a kind of optical illusion of his consciousness."

— ALBERT EINSTEIN

You, like every other person on the planet, are both an individual mortal being as well as an eternal soul with a consciousness who's a part of the larger universal consciousness. When you're embracing wholeliness, you identify with the latter and recognize your sacred, healing connections to all: the Divine, your guardian angels, the spirits who are watching over you, the cosmos, nature, and all people and creatures. You can always call on any of these entities for assistance, and they will answer you.

Whenever you're aware of your true nature, you're better able to experience fulfillment, harmony, and courage. You're also more creative, and you'll see possibilities and opportunities that would elude your awareness if you were stuck in the grip of your ego and its endless fears.

On the other hand, when you are only aware of your physical self and turn away from wholeliness—thinking that it's a nice idea but a fantasy—you feel lost, forlorn, and adrift in a cruel and uncaring world. You actually create your own hell by allowing your individual ego to take control of your consciousness.

Hell is the false perception that you're separate from the Divine and the sacred healing connections to all of its manifestations—all of the loving, creative forces of the universe. In literature and religion, hell has been portrayed as a realm of damnation inhabited by those sinful souls who were denied the right to enter heaven. This is a highly imaginative and figurative interpretation, yet hell is very real: you create it when you stop believing that you're part of universal consciousness and instead let your ego control your actions.

The word *ego* comes from the Latin word for *I*. We all have an ego because we all have a sense of ourselves as individuals. Therefore, whenever you perceive yourself as separate, you're "in your ego," and it can become so dominant that it takes over and blocks your vision of your true nature.

This perspective has its positive aspects, however. It allows you to be aware of what's special about you and helps you tend to your safety and survival needs as a mortal being. If you had no ego, you wouldn't have the ability to look out for yourself, so it's essential to a certain degree.

But the ego is not supposed to be your only identity, dominating your consciousness at all times. Wholeliness is about balance, including the balance between your individual identity and your identity as part of the whole. When you forget who you are, as a soul eternally intertwined in the fabric of life, your ego takes you to a hellish state of disconnection.

Your ego often functions as a persistently pessimistic voice in your head, for it has an irrational fear of losing its own identity, and for good reason. Who would you be if you weren't an individual with your own memories, ideas, perceptions, and talents? What would happen to you if your consciousness were completely subsumed by the universal consciousness? The ego is obsessed with such questions.

What your ego doesn't understand, though, is that those aspects of who you are will always be attached your immortal soul.

They're not going anywhere! Even after death, you won't forget that thrilling moment when you first met your life partner and realized you were in love. You'll still retain your propensity toward reflection that draws others to you for advice, or your sense of humor that lightens the burden when you and your friends are feeling dejected and need to be uplifted. Never forget that you remain who you are, with all your gifts, when you recognize wholeliness and your part in the collective consciousness.

Ego-based fear is irrational. You can find a wonderful balance between the ego and the bigger whole in which both sides shine and neither is lost to the other. When you see that, it's easier to quiet the anxiety generated by the ego and embrace wholeliness.

The Ego's Purpose

The most basic purpose of the ego is survival. Humans have been equipped with a powerful survival instinct for good reason: Early on in our development as a species, we spent most of our time simply trying to stay alive in a harsh landscape. Using intuition and rational abilities, we discovered tools, fire, and social bonding. All of these made it much easier to avoid danger or death.

In order to survive, we needed to rely on a physical mechanism that would ensure we could react quickly to protect our bodies in times of danger. As a result, the human brain was designed to make note of what appears to be a threat and automatically trigger the parasympathetic nervous system to create a response of "fight or flight." In the presence of perceived threat (which isn't always real), the body behaves by increasing the heart rate. Breathing becomes shallow, and the brain tells the glands to release stress hormones into the bloodstream. All of these instant physiological reactions give humans the power to run away quickly and find a hiding spot or fight for our lives.

Modern humans are hardwired to use our intuitive and cognitive abilities to adapt to difficult conditions and a changing environment. We still have the strength of those who endured the Ice Age, yet emotionally, we experience the fight-or-flight phenomenon as fear. In truly perilous situations, there's no time to think; we have to move fast!

Just like so many of us, you're probably in the habit of thinking too much about potential threats. Fight or flight is supposed to be a short-lived, rarely used safety mechanism for emergencies only. Yet if you see an advertisement or TV show designed to scare you into action, or your friend makes a disrespectful comment, your ego will generate a sense of danger, and your body will respond accordingly. Your negative and fearful thoughts will set off the chain reaction of the fight-or-flight syndrome, just as if you were caught outside in a terrible storm or being chased by a wild animal.

In reality, the "danger" may be only in your mind. So what if you could stop this instantaneous response and use your willpower to help you break the habit of giving in to this insecurity? Imagine how much less stressful your life would be.

The ego is able to create a false sense of vulnerability very quickly. As you let it dominate your awareness, your mind will generate thoughts that justify this fear and embellish it. At the core of cognitive therapy, which I use with my clients, is the recognition that our minds will quickly discard any evidence that we're safe, blowing out of proportion the smallest bit of evidence that we're in danger.

Once this reaction has been triggered, you start to think about frightening situations from the past, or ones that might occur in the future. The possibilities of "danger" seem to be everywhere! As a result, your body begins to remain in the fight-or-flight response for longer periods of time, never calming down and trusting that you're safe and supported by others. Worry, fear, and the anger that accompanies them begin to eat away at your health and well-being. Additionally, stress can bring on a whole host of diseases, such as mental disorders, gastrointestinal problems, chronic pain, and even cancer. These detrimental effects will only stop once you learn to check your ego.

Egotism and Narcissism

When you're ruled by your ego, every day seems as if it's filled with struggles and conflicts, because you're chronically scared. After a while, you become so overwhelmed that you start to run away from any situation that might be emotionally challenging. You perceive the world as a terrible place where you're treated poorly and only the most aggressive competitors survive. The mind responds in predictable ways, and your view of reality becomes distorted.

Once you become obsessed with your safety, or you falsely believe that you're in control of your world—and therefore can avoid suffering—your problems begin in earnest. You start to forget about the security and happiness of those around you . . . and you slowly creep toward narcissism and controlling, arrogant behavior. This is painful to admit, but keep in mind that egotism and fear are part of being human.

Look around you, and you'll see many people who appear to be self-righteous, smug, or condescending—but upon closer examination, they're utterly terrified. Their egos are dominating their thinking, and fear and anger rule their hearts. According to the book of Revelation in the Bible, Satan was once an angel of God, but then his untamed ego led him to create a battle for control, and he was thrown down from the heavens. This is a metaphor for how we let the unchecked ego drag us into a self-created hell.

Someone who's in a state of narcissism sees everybody and everything as a potential tool for building up his own safety or as a threat. Brotherhood is impossible, for he finds himself unable to treat others as equals. To do so would be to cede the illusion of control. In some cases, the narcissist is so disconnected from his higher self, or immortal soul, that he feels no remorse about having mistreated others, and his mind finds ways to justify his behavior. Thankfully, most people are not to this point, since they have *some* awareness of wholeliness. They possess at least an inkling of the idea that life is not a battle for survival, but is a cooperative effort for evolving and expressing the creative force of the Divine, bringing them to the point that they instinctively question this "me against the world" mentality. Feelings of guilt and sadness arise when they mistreat others, and these emotions are gifts from the Divine designed to awaken them to wholeliness, the cure for fear and egotism.

Your conscience is the voice of your immortal soul. It calls you to embrace wholeliness, stop creating bad karma, and return to a wholesome way of living. The Divine—and all the spirits who watch over and love you—will send you message after message meant to awaken you to your sacred, healing connections. Spirit wants you to return to the fold, to paradise, instead of wandering adrift in a lonely and barren desert of the ego where there's no nourishment, fulfillment, or happiness.

In the Bible, Jesus tells the parable of the prodigal son. The message is that no matter how far our egos take us away from God, He loves us unconditionally and wants to bring us back to a state of security, love, protection, and joy; He doesn't want to scold or punish us. As represented by the father of the prodigal son, the Divine wishes for us to return to his loving, protective arms and end our self-created suffering. We can't do this when we're being led around by our egos.

• • •

Narcissism is like poison. It creates a sense of loneliness so powerful that people will turn to anything—drugs, sexual exploitation of others, or manipulative and cruel games—to distract themselves from the horrible feeling of being alone. Whenever you see this behavior in others, find your compassion for the good soul within that suffering individual. And when you see egotism in yourself, banish it and forgive yourself. Reconnect to the Divine through prayer and meditation. Ask to feel the holy, healing presence of Spirit.

To help humanity change, to strengthen yourself and experience power and peace, you must calm your overreacting survival instinct that sees danger everywhere and tempts you to turn to narcissism and denial. Meditation and regular exercise can slow this panic response, but nothing will eliminate it completely (which is good, since it provides protection in the case of real danger). You have to learn to resist lashing out or running away simply because your brain too often instantly responds to events with fear. Mentally note when you're feeling fear, and use your mind to explore whether this emotion is actually justified or simply an automatic, distorted response to an event.

The Shadow of the Psyche

Deep in the psyche, far from the light of conscious awareness, are beliefs that feed the ego's fear and keep it overactive. Psychologist Carl Jung explained that everyone's ego has a shadow, where all the uncomfortable truths and beliefs about themselves lie hidden. Such thoughts or feelings become stashed in a dark attic, metaphorically speaking, because of the pain they cause.

Believing that we're inadequate or unintelligent can make us very sad, angry, or ashamed. The ego should help us examine that idea, where it came from, and whether it's true. Instead, driven by fear, it buries it in the shadow. There in the subconscious mind, the belief actually gains more power to increase the ego's fear and anger because our conscious mind isn't aware of it or able to see it for what it is: a destructive thought that we need to heal.

If you rummage around in the shadow of your subconscious, and choose to shine the light of love and awareness on the dark corners of your memory, you're likely to illuminate what has caused you pain. Often these beliefs are false, but should they turn out to be true, you can nevertheless find the gift in them.

Perhaps you'll become aware that deep inside, you believe that you're not as smart as those around you. The light of awareness could expose this as false: you might discover that you are intelligent after all. Then again, you may find that you aren't "intelligent" in the traditional sense, but you're quite brilliant in your own way. Maybe you aren't meant to be a scholar yourself, but to use your talent for entertaining and encouraging others to inspire scholars when they're feeling frustrated.

All of us have many gifts, so there's no reason to feel ashamed if we have one set of talents and not another. Love illuminates, so as we lovingly examine the thoughts we've hidden in our subconscious mind, our insights will be colored by compassion rather than judgment.

Whatever your own beliefs may be, they mustn't remain caged within your shadow. They should always be brought to the surface, explored, and resolved. Bringing light to the shadow helps you discard the untruths that make you feel ashamed, unworthy, or afraid others will discover that you're inferior and inadequate. You aren't any of these things! At the same time, this light of awareness will expose those good qualities that got lost in your "attic": your beauty, your value, your power, or whatever it is that you've convinced yourself isn't something you possess.

To embrace wholeliness is to reconnect what's in the shadows with your conscious awareness. You carry a flashlight into the dark corners of the mind in order to find hidden treasures and shed light on old, broken pieces of furniture (emotions). Perhaps these were inherited from your parents or grandparents, and now that you've found them, you're determined to put them where they belong: in the junkyard!

If you start to clean out the attic of your mind, you can get rid of what you don't need and bring back the wonderful qualities you forgot or didn't realize you had. A sense of wholeliness and healing will arise in you because you've returned to yourself what was missing: beautiful characteristics that are like precious treasures.

The shadow and its secrets feed the ego's fear, so you must begin to tame the beast within. Like the Greek mythological character Theseus, you must go deep within the labyrinth to face the Minotaur, the terrible creature that dwells inside you, which is the only way to slay him. He won't go away unless you venture into the darkness.

How do you accomplish this? With compassion and understanding. Then, like in a fairy tale, the Minotaur can be transformed into the prince or hero who rescues you. This beast, your out-of-control ego, is subdued by your inner ability to face your fears and bring light into the hidden corners of your awareness. By confronting head-on the issues that you've suppressed, you may find the Minotaur not so difficult to slay after all.

Group Ego

When we're in danger, our hardwiring often tells us to fight or flee, as I explained earlier. But it can also cause us to gather in groups and work together to solve problems, which is also a form of self-protection. This mentality ensured the survival of early humans because they could pool their resources. Looking out for the group meant looking out for themselves as individuals.

Whenever you perceive a division between a faction you belong to and another faction, you're experiencing group ego simply by identifying with your own. You are, in effect, saying that to survive you have to ensure that those whom you associate with dominate all others.

In this state, your concern is only for yourself and your faction (you don't see a difference between your needs and those of the group). This collection of people might be your family, the department you work for within a company, those you share an ethnicity or religion with, and so on. Whatever it is, anyone who isn't part of your group is foreign, and you eye him with suspicion. You only allow yourself to see differences—and when you do, fear arises, and you instantly find yourself wary of "the other." Unfortunately, you become very cautious around these "aliens" (it's interesting that we often use the same term to refer to immigrants and foreigners that we use to describe extraterrestrial beings who "invade" Earth!) and start to believe that, just as you see them as the enemy, they must view *your* group in the same way.

However, in a state of wholeliness, you're able to keep your group and personal egos in check. You have a sense of personal identity, but don't necessarily assume that you're better or more important. You're aware of a group identity without accepting the idea that yours is superior. Within the wholeliness mind-set, you see common ground between yourself and others, regardless of what classifications may be involved.

• • •

Group ego is instinctual. If you walk into a social gathering, you instinctively glance around to see what other people are wearing or doing (Are you overdressed or underdressed?) and whether you seem to fit in (Are they all drinking? Talking politics? Watching a sporting event on TV?). You immediately look to see if you know anyone. If you don't, you scan the room for someone who looks approachable—someone who looks like you or seems to share a common interest. We *all* do this.

The danger with this manifestation of the ego is that if you don't catch yourself when you're feeling anxious or suspicious—and consciously choose to change your thought processes—your behavior can become destructive and evolve into a form of narcissism. You might start to think that you're being protective; but in actuality, you're only seeking to exclude those who are not a part of your group. At the root of this behavior is your fear and desire to better your own chances of survival by being a part of something more powerful than yourself. You know your "tribe" will support you, so you want it to be strong.

In reality, group ego is divisive. It makes you think, *I'm better than you are because my people are better than your people.* Genocide and war are extreme results of this mentality, but you experience it in your own life. It might be that you don't want to get to know your neighbors because you think their values aren't as good as yours are. Or you could be on the receiving end of someone else's group ego: perhaps your child has been bullied in school because he's seen as "different."

To stop participating in this behavior—and, as an extension, creating bad karma—you have to remember that at the bottom of an egotistical thought is fear. You may not feel as if you'd be afraid of a person who is different, but the ego disguises this emotion by turning it into self-righteous anger or judgment in order to feel powerful, important, and superior. So keep in mind that whenever you're self-righteous or hostile toward others, what you're actually experiencing is fear.

It's hard to admit to such ugly behavior, but every single one of us falls into the ego's grip at times. We become afraid that we're different, that the group we associate with secretly judges us as inferior, and we act out negatively. This fear is the beast within, which we all must conquer with love.

The Victim Mentality

Having an active group ego will also cause you to identify too much with the problems you face, tempting you into developing the "victim mentality." Instead of thinking about how you have power in every situation in your life (even if it's only the power to choose your attitude), you start obsessing about your powerlessness.

Ultimately, this disposition is divisive and destructive; and unfortunately, it's also quite prevalent these days. Due to all of the advances in communication technology, we have instant access to other groups. We're now able to see other people and their differences with more frequency, which triggers our egos.

When caught up in group ego, individuals tend to blame outside factors for their problems instead of examining their own ability to address them. For example, in the U.S. we use more than our fair share of energy compared with much of the rest of the world. But if I were to mention this to a fellow American in conversation, she is likely to point her finger at China, India, or any other nation that's guilty of high energy usage. If we must conserve the earth's resources, the reasoning goes, that group *over there* has to start first!

It's much easier to deflect criticism by condemning others rather than looking at ourselves and saying, "Is this criticism true? Can I do better? Can I help my group do better?" Life isn't a competition for who has the better story of being misunderstood, unappreciated, or mistreated. Excuses for our behavior keep us locked in the same stagnant pattern.

Wholeliness is the balm that eases the fear and anxiety that's making you miserable. It allows you to balance your many identities: as an individual, a member of many different groups, and a part of creation. It reminds you that even people you don't know are looking out for you (because they believe in wholeliness, too), while affirming that you have a responsibility to look out for them as well. Better yet, it helps you find the courage to trust and reach out to others, even if there's a chance of getting hurt. This wonderful state of being connected and supported transforms you on the inside, making it far easier for you to change your behaviors. It keeps your personal and group egos in check so that they perform their proper functions instead of dominating your consciousness with irrational emotions.

Inevitably, you'll find that it's tiring to constantly conform to the expectations of your group and compete with others. There's no reason to carry the burden of seeing everyone as rivals. Know that it's possible to love your groups and think that they're "the best" without putting down those of others. If you respect other religions, races, opinions, and ideas, then you'll help manifest wholeliness on Earth.

Individualistic and Collective Societies: A Balance

Group ego shows up in every type of society, but at this point all of us have to find a balance between the needs of the self and the needs of the group, between the desires of our own small group and those of the larger whole. We have to stop being divisive and egotistical. Only then will societies evolve as they should.

Generally speaking, there are two types of human societies: individualistic and collective. America is an individualist society, whereas many Asian and Latin American countries are collectivist. Americans value a person who is unique, works for himself, and is self-made—and all of these are wonderful qualities. However, in this type of society, it's easy to give in to egotism. People can be shockingly blind to the help they've received from parents, their community, teachers, police officers, their government, and their environment. It's sad, but when there's too much emphasis on individualism, it's easy take for granted the blessings of being part of a larger group.

On the other hand, collectivist cultures expect people to work well in groups and cooperate for the betterment of the whole. Compliance is rewarded with protection, but the downside can be that there tends to be less personal freedom. Further, it can be difficult for individuals to express themselves without feeling as if they're somehow betraying the group or harming the whole.

With freedom, which is cherished in the West, comes responsibility and the need to tolerate difference. People who come from societies that have been built on conformity can be very uncomfortable with the diversity they find in an individualistic culture. If they're not open to this drastic change, group ego can begin to creep in.

Obviously, there are pros and cons to both systems. When I was in my 20s living in Romania, all my friends' families had a home, a car, and jobs; and while no one had great material wealth or possessions that stood out from anyone else's, we were content. We didn't have the extremes of rich and poor that are seen in capitalist countries, but we also didn't have the opportunity to climb the social ladder. Now that I've lived in both societies, I think the problem is the lack of ego balance among individuals and groups—which goes way beyond how a government rules a nation. If people embrace wholeliness, any weaknesses and flaws will be counteracted because it creates harmony instead of discord, competition, or egotism.

Wholeliness can open our eyes to new ways of working together. Perhaps all that we've accomplished so far will make way for the new era of human consciousness and be seen as obsolete compared with the much better systems we'll invent that are in sync with Divine law.

Why Group Ego Gets Out of Control

Whenever a group we're a part of becomes very large, we start to feel lost, and suspicion and distrust can arise. In a small company, church, or social group, for example, it's easier to know the members and trust that everyone is honest and has integrity. But when a group is larger, members will often create subgroups within it in order to feel more secure. It's hard for people to perceive and embrace wholeliness when they feel that their institutions are too powerful to be influenced by individuals. As companies grow, governments expand, and the earth's population explodes, it's only natural that we start to feel powerless up against these immense systems.

At the same time, technology is making us increasingly aware of just how many humans are on this planet. But the fear that we're becoming lost in the larger whole can be alleviated by wholeliness, which involves understanding the balance between our individual ego, the group ego, and our identity as an integral part of creation. Wholeliness allows us to believe that we can transform the whole by making changes at the grassroots level. We start to realize that, while we as individuals don't have the ability to end world hunger, each of us can work to make a difference by feeding homeless people in our own communities. When our perceptions shift, we start to do our small part to heal the planet, while discovering firsthand that we're not alone. As this occurs, we see that there are others who are willing to support and assist us when we need it most.

Your judgments will begin to change very quickly once you increase your awareness of how much influence your ego has had over you. As you become more skilled at recognizing its intentions, you'll embrace your ability to keep it in check and live in a state of wholeliness instead of divisiveness, love instead of fear and suspicion, and faith instead of cynicism.

How to Overcome the Ego's Resistance to Wholeliness

Observe

In your journal, make a list of the groups you feel a part of and the words that describe you as a member of a group. You might say, "I am an Asian female baby boomer, a San Franciscan, a member of the local running group and the Unity Church," and so on. Think of as many associations that you're a part of as possible.

Next, write out all the positive qualities of these groups. What do you like about being identified with them? What about them makes you feel safe, secure, and like you belong?

Then consider all of their negative qualities, and notice whether it's easier to make this list than it was to make the previous one. Do you feel good about all of your groups? Are you embarrassed or uncomfortable being affiliated with some of them but proud to belong to others? Do certain ones behave in ways that contradict wholeliness?

Now observe how you exhibit the positive and negative qualities of your groups. Have you ever met someone outside of them who shares the positive qualities you embody as a member? Think about this. Why is it that a person who is nurturing, passionate, dedicated, and so on is not a part of your group? Can you see the connection between you and that individual?

Imagine other people who have these wonderful qualities. Who are they? How can you connect with them?

Finally, look at the negative qualities you listed. Say to yourself, "I am [list the quality], and I love myself. I trust that others will help me heal this aspect of myself. I am healing it even now."

Pray

Pray for help in healing the negative qualities within yourself and to find their positive aspects. Ask for help in finding the good attributes you don't think you have, and to feel secure about whatever it is you think you possess. Request that the Divine show you your many beautiful gifts.

Seek assistance in being more loving, accepting, and understanding of those who are different from you. Pray that you will be open to opportunities for spreading love and compassion, while also welcoming these emotions into your heart. Ask Spirit to banish your fears and open your mind so that you may find the commonalities between you and those who may seem different.

Act

To share a meal with others is to remind yourself of your connection to all of life, as eating and socializing is something all humans have done throughout the course of history. Make a point of dining with people who are from a group you're not a part of, one that makes you somewhat uncomfortable because you don't know much about them. Remember that it's okay to be a bit uncomfortable—it's a sign that you're trying to evolve!

During this meal, listen and ask lots of questions. Think about the commonalities you share. Do all of you at the table have children? Do you live in the same city or work for the same company? As you talk about your experiences, look for shared aims with the others at the table.

I promise that you have at least five things in common with each person in the room; try to discover them.

You may want to turn this event into a regular activity. For instance, once a month you might get together for a simple meal. You could also have lunch together in a restaurant; if you do, rotate the neighborhood and cuisine you choose so that no one feels excluded. This way, you'll begin to overcome your feelings of isolation and separation that are the result of the individual and group ego dividing people.

Before and after each meal, reflect on the simple grace of being able to enjoy the fruits of the earth with others. Thank the Divine for the presence of those who make this world a beautiful place to live.

Enjoying graceful dining experiences with others and sharing joy, laughter, and hopes for tomorrow has become a lost art. As you reclaim them, consider what else you've lost in your ego's quest for power. What have you overlooked in your busy life? What simple pleasures have escaped you? How have you fostered your own disconnection and isolation—not just from other groups, but from the individuals in your own life? Do your family members all retreat to different areas of the house to eat dinner in front of a computer screen or television? Do you know what's going on in each other's lives?

Make a commitment to share meals and conversation. It will help you balance your perception so you'll never forget that you're both an individual and a member of a larger whole, and that both identities are equally important.

In Part II, you will learn about the many sacred connections your ego has caused you to overlook, ones that will help you draw upon all the loving support that's always available. As you begin to understand these connections—and give them credence even when your senses attempt to fool you into thinking that they aren't real after all—you will start to experience wholeliness. There will be times when you feel you're perfectly in union with all; cherish this experience! Recognize that in these moments you're aware of the true nature of reality. Embrace this ideal state so that you can begin to bring wholeliness to this earthly realm.

•• ● ••

PART II

SACRED CONNECTIONS

WHOLELINESS AND THE VISIBLE WORLD

*"When we try to pick out anything by itself,
we find it hitched to everything else
in the universe."*

— JOHN MUIR

There's a saying from Hermeticism: "As above, so below." The shapes, actions, and natures of objects in the material world echo each other. There are similarities between galaxies, human beings, and cells. Therefore, you as a person are not so different from your cells or the Milky Way! As cell biologist Bruce Lipton, Ph.D., wrote in his book *The Biology of Belief:* "[Cells] *retreated* from toxins that I introduced into the culture dish, just as humans retreat from mountain lions and muggers in dark alleys. They also *gravitated* to nutrients, just as humans gravitate to breakfast, lunch, dinner, and love." No matter its size, everything that is part of the whole moves, changes, and affects the other parts.

Although we tend to overlook such remarkable connections in the modern era, the ancients were well aware that we're woven into the natural world that we live in. They recognized the sacred, healing connection all human beings have to the world of our senses. Healers, shamans, wise elders, and philosophers understood that just like our planet, the human body is composed mostly of water, and that the moon affects the tides as well as women's menstrual cycles. Thanks to their careful study of the stars and the seasons, our ancestors were able to invent calendars and scientific theories for predicting cycles and events, even those thousands of years into the future. They came up with complex systems of astrology and discovered sacred geometry and the power of numbers, which led to the development of numerology.

The best scientists and engineers still scratch their heads over how pyramids were designed and constructed by "primitive" people in Egypt, Mexico, and South America so long ago. They're baffled by how heavy stones, including those that were shaped into huge obelisks, were transported many miles from quarries and used to create monuments. They're also curious about why these civilizations felt that it was so important to build these extraordinary structures. Were they monuments to the egos of kings and pharaohs, or were they perhaps symbols for the sacred connections between the natural world, Spirit, and humans?

Wisdom didn't simply come from people's own observations of the natural world; it also came from the hidden knowledge that they accessed through prayer, meditation, and other methods of interacting with a Higher Power. The ancients utilized Divine influence when creating their wondrous structures, as well as in conceiving theories that have withstood the test of time as great intellectual achievements. One possible explanation for this is that they didn't see the brain as the seat of all knowledge. In fact, when the Egyptians carefully prepared the body of a dead pharaoh for his next existence, they preserved all the inner organs except the brain, which they threw out! Yet today we think of the human mind as a powerful calculating machine that generates all the useful information we'll ever need. While it's true that our brains are full of potential that we've yet to even tap, much of that capacity lies in our ability to make use of our sacred connections and draw in the knowledge that's available to us through the collective consciousness.

The beliefs about our minds functioning like machines are beginning to change, however. One reason is that neurologists are helping us see that we've been thinking too mechanistically, underestimating the intricacy of the natural world and the connections between seemingly disparate events. They're discovering that many parts of the brain are simultaneously operating during everyday tasks, such as speaking, reading, or listening to music. The complexities we're discovering in the human experience reflect the complexities in nature and the cosmos. We're beginning to accept that what happens on one part of the planet influences another, even if we don't quite see or understand how this is happening. Often, the correlation is invisible.

We're also realizing that ecosystems are far more complicated, with far more interconnections between species of plants and animals, than we ever imagined. When we introduce a foreign species of fungus into a river or lake, for instance—or eliminate a species we find troublesome, such as wolves or certain insects—the effects are far greater than we anticipated. The lesson here is that we have to look at the whole and recognize that the entire ecosystem is complete, balanced, and in harmony with itself. It does not need to be tinkered with, and we disturb that balance at our own peril.

Our bodies' similarities to the systems of the natural world, and our interconnectedness with them, can't be denied. For example, we can easily upset our own balance by treating a symptom with a pharmaceutical drug that has effects on other areas we didn't anticipate. Even drinking too much water can throw off our electrolytes and the harmony within the whole. We are continually upsetting the state of health within our own bodies because we're not looking at the totality of ourselves, nature, and the cosmos. We fail to recognize the fundamental truth that everything is connected.

Reclaiming the Wisdom of Our Sacred Connections

When we look at the remarkably accurate Mayan calendar that was developed thousands of years ago, or we read the writings of Indian mystics or ancient Greek philosophers, our current understanding of our relationship to the cosmos and the natural world seems paltry by comparison. We have plenty of *knowledge* about the reality we perceive with our senses, but lack the *wisdom* that comes from the perspective of wholeliness. We are in the habit of seeing only part of the picture, not the totality, and rely entirely too much on information without placing an emphasis on how it all fits together.

While science has brought marvelous advancements to the human experience, we've lost touch with the older wisdom that would put this "new" knowledge into context. In the era of evolution that we're currently in, we must reclaim what we've forgotten. We must go beyond science—which offers a limited view of our connections to the visible world—and relearn the lessons that the heavens and the earth have given us.

Ayurvedic teachings and healing techniques, which originated in India, are based on the idea that our bodies echo the four elements of nature—earth, air, fire, and water—as well as ether, or Spirit. Wicca, an old religion of Europe, also emphasizes these five elements united by Spirit. Chinese astrology recognizes basically the same five elements (it recognizes metal instead of Spirit) and associates them with particular planets and animals. (For example, Mercury is associated with water and the black tortoise.) Ancient civilizations from all corners of the globe once acknowledged these sacred connections, but modern humans have been conditioned to believe that these ideas are "primitive" and inferior to scientific understanding. Yet science can't explain many phenomena, such as healing the body through the power of the mind, despite the frequency with which they occur.

Being conscious of all relationships opens our eyes to our interactions with the cosmos, nature, and the realm beyond the senses where the spirits of those who have passed dwell, which we'll discuss later. Right now, let's take a closer look at our connections to the visible world so that we can more easily understand this concept of wholeliness.

Disconnected from Nature, Plugged into Technology

Unlike early humans, who depended on knowledge of the stars, weather patterns, and natural events for their very survival, you probably look to technology to guide you. Recently, I was outdoors with some friends in the evening, and someone asked, "What's that bright star up there in the sky?" Immediately, three people pulled out their smartphones, activated an application, held these devices to the sky, and pronounced that it was Venus! Soon, they were pointing out many constellations. This is a marvelous use of technology to connect with the night sky, but if you're indoors and want to know whether it's raining, do you walk over to the nearest window, or do you consult a website or an application? When was the last time you appreciated the power of a grand thunderstorm or saw wildlife in its natural setting?

Our ancestors had to invent techniques to better understand the rhythms of their world. For example, their lives depended on being conscious of the growing season. Or if they were mariners, they had to carefully calculate the positions of the stars to know which direction they were sailing. Today, we may be able to simply glance at the GPS on our car's dashboard to see where we are, but most of us don't even know how these technologies work. Even so, such devices have become integral to our existence, and we depend on them to make our lives more convenient.

Most of us have forgotten what it's like to rely on our knowledge and experience of the world to stay safe, and we find ourselves feeling very inconvenienced whenever the Internet connection goes down. Because we live in an environment of artificial lighting, heating, and cooling, we don't pay very much attention to the earth, water, or sky. Our lives aren't based upon knowing the activities of our surroundings but on an intangible "cyber" world. We have such limited contact with nature that we don't comprehend our relationship with this huge entity that encompasses microscopic bacteria, insects, birds, trees, forests, ecosystems, planets, and galaxies.

From our current perspective, it's hard for us to imagine that events in the cosmos might interrupt our everyday communications, but we'll see more of this happening as we go through a critical time of transformation and evolution in the next several years. Don't be surprised if one day you find that you and everyone you know is without cell-phone coverage, or you discover your bank account has gone missing because a force of nature caused the huge network to shut down! Crises such as these will all be part of a Divine wake-up call to stop being absorbed in our egos and technologies and remember our sacred connections to the larger whole of the earth and human existence.

The Web of Life

If primitive ideas about the planets influencing us seem quaint or fanciful, it's because we don't understand wholeliness and our relationship with the cosmos. Many people have heard of the Pythagorean theory of *the music of the spheres,* and think of it merely as a poetic way of describing the movements of the planets. In reality, the ratios that the Greeks identified with the planets' movements have musical significance, for they mirror musical intervals that, according to Elena Mannes's *The Power of Music: Pioneering Discoveries in the New Science of Song,* are the very musical intervals people around the globe are most likely to identify as pleasant and melodic. In addition, scientists have found that we can use harmonious sounds to soothe our minds and improve our moods. Certain types of music can even stimulate or relax us when we're in the womb, for we're attuned to music before we're born. Thus, the music of the spheres is real, and it's another example of how we're affected by the visible world.

Despite our disconnection from nature, it's a vital part of the visible world that is our home—and its number one lesson for us is wholeliness. As the American Indian Chief Seattle said, "Humankind has not woven the web of life. We are but one thread within it. Whatever we do to the web, we do to ourselves. All things are bound together. All things connect." Thus if we disturb one thread, we are disturbing our own as well.

Nature, like the cosmos and ourselves, is in a constant state of transformation. Species die off and new ones develop. However, we're imposing too many changes in too short a period of time, and the planet is having trouble adapting to our powerful influences. We've quadrupled our population in just 100 years, but the earth hasn't created more land, water, or sky to accommodate our rise in numbers. Also, as our race has multiplied, we've begun to hinder the survival of other living things. Ironically, as human life increases, more species of creatures, plants, and trees have disappeared. What if one of these species held the key for curing cancer, autism, or Alzheimer's disease?

The lesson here for us is twofold: First, we must be aware that our cumulative influence on the planet is great, so we have to make better choices about how to interact with it. Second, we have to recognize that our seemingly inconsequential actions influence our families, communities, environment, and world; that is, *all* of life. Even the smallest positive action is better than no action at all.

When you choose to embrace wholeliness and respect and value your sacred connections, you live up to your responsibility and find yourself acting in ways that are supportive of the whole. You think about where your food comes from and where your garbage goes. You realize that when you conserve water, electricity, and fuel, you're contributing to the sustainability of your home. As a result, you feel a sense of peace and power as you do what you can to ensure that you don't exploit the earth's resources, for you know that your gentle treatment of the planet contributes to the health and well-being of all people and all creatures.

Gaia, Our Mother Earth

The "Gaia theory" puts forth the notion that the earth has consciousness, that it's best understood as an organism with all its creatures and plants as part of its living, breathing body. Some ancient civilizations of the world went as far as to anthropomorphize Gaia as a big-breasted female figure with large thighs, the shape of a very fertile human woman (a little body fat on a woman enhances her ability to become pregnant).

If you imagine the earth as a being, it can help you understand and appreciate the nature of your own system. As I mentioned, the earth is mostly water, as are we—so, just as you don't want to become dehydrated or allow your bodily fluids to become contaminated with toxins, you wouldn't want the planet to be drained of its wonderful resource of freshwater. The earth has layers of atmosphere, and if one is harmed (for instance, if there's a hole in the ozone), it affects the whole. Similarly, a human being is a system with many invisible links, one of which is a connection to an etheric body that contains seven energy centers, or *chakras*. The chakras are like funnels of energy attached along the spine, with the top two extending outward from your head. If one of them is unhealthy, the dark and heavy energy that's causing it to function improperly will affect the physical body, polluting it and potentially causing illness and disease.

It's imperative that we all embrace wholeliness and heal our relationship with Mother Earth. We want to keep her healthy and thriving. Sadly, we tax her just as a spoiled child might drain the energy of his own mother. We make unreasonable demands, insult her, and mistreat her. We destroy huge areas of forests, oceans, and grasslands, assuming that she can tolerate our abuse. What we don't always realize is that natural disasters are a violent release of the earth's negative emotions. No wonder she's rebelling and releasing tension and energy through earthquakes, tsunamis, and hurricanes. Her patience is wearing thin!

• • •

When you have a rash, even if it covers only a portion of your body, it's still something that you want to address and cure. Almost instinctively, you look for the underlying cause and ask, "Why is my skin breaking out? What's being brought into my body that's acting like a toxin and causing this reaction?" You don't ignore the problem and focus on the parts of you that appear healthy.

Of course in certain regions of the world, people's behaviors are worse than in others, just as a rash is worse in some areas of the body compared with others. Similarly, we have to stop kidding ourselves and saying, "We're in pretty good shape as a species. Look at the people of a higher consciousness who are treating the earth and each other well." The fact is that there are entirely too many individuals of lower consciousness acting very destructively, and that must change. No matter how minor our contribution may seem, each of us must play a part in healing the world and raising human awareness.

Perhaps you live in an area that's known as a cancer "hot spot" because of the unusually high number of cases among inhabitants. You can choose to make an extra effort to get cancer screenings and live more healthfully, but you can do even more to help yourself and your neighbors. You can get involved in learning more about why the disease rate is so high in the area. Are there carcinogenic fertilizers being sprayed on lawns, trees, and bushes? Are people consuming large amounts of toxins, or using cleaning supplies laden with chemicals? You can decide to lead a more natural lifestyle and avoid such products, but you can also encourage those in your community to do the same so that you, your children, and your pets live healthier lives and walk more softly upon the earth. You can increase your commitment to be kinder to Mother Earth and educate and inspire others to do the same.

Being Kind to Our Mother

Unfortunately, our planet is not an object that constantly re-generates resources for us at the rate we use them. We're being selfish and disrespectful, upsetting its balance and harmony. Currently, certain energy companies are extracting natural gas from underground sources by pumping millions of gallons of chemically contaminated water at very high pressure into the rock below the surface, which results in explosions. Propane is then released and collected, but the engineers can't possibly control the effects of the damage being done to what they can't see. It is known that gas and chemicals are entering groundwater and contaminating it. And if the earth were a sentient creature, who would inject it with poison and expect it to heal from such a violent assault?

There are people who feel that this is acceptable behavior because they don't have the vision to imagine ways we might more gently make use of the planet's resources by limiting our need for power and fuel. Indeed, humans have thought of only the most invasive and ravaging ways to extract the natural resources that we've been provided. It's time to lend a loving hand to Mother Earth in her recovery back to health and balance. For even as she is struggling with the burden of caring for us, she continues to offer us her powers.

The water, air, and sky are all conduits for the Divine to heal. When life became unbalanced for the ancient people of the world, going to sacred hills, waters, and mountains bestowed peace and healing upon them. Illness or disharmony of the spirit, mind, or body could be cured in holy places where the connection to Spirit was especially easy to make. Yet nature's powers are still available to humans today.

Have you ever walked in nature and felt as if the leaves and branches were reaching out to you? Next time you're outside, hear the sounds of birds everywhere, the buzzing of cicadas, and know that Gaia is doing her job, busily creating and sustaining life. Maybe there's a spot where you feel especially aware of the Divine presence, the support of your loved ones who have passed and those who are here to help you. Do you go to it often, or do you find that you're too busy? This may be your sacred healing location, whether it's your backyard, a nearby lake, or a mountain meadow filled with wildflowers.

Settings in nature inspire our lives when we're struggling to find meaning; they reconnect us to the greater network of the Divine. It's deeply comforting to know that the earth is always there for us—just as the Divine is—loving, healing, and creating energy that can renew our lives. Research has shown that spending time outdoors not only affects our moods for the better, it can also boost immunity, reduce depression and symptoms of ADHD, and lower blood pressure.

Recently, scientists have discovered the importance of sunlight in the creation of serotonin, our "feel good" hormone, and vitamin D, which is vital for health . . . yet we've ignored Grandma's prescription for "plenty of fresh air and sunshine." We live by fluorescent lights and electronic equipment, and then wonder why we feel unfocused and disconnected. In fact, we've forgotten that the best medicine is nature, something that the Divine provides (I'll talk more about this later in the book).

It's now up to every single one of us to begin the process of change. Do we really need *every* modern convenience we're used to? Do we need our products to be packaged so heavily? Do we need so many material goods that end up in landfills and create so much pollution when they're manufactured and shipped? We are straining Mother Earth's resources, and for what? Supposedly, when Socrates walked through the marketplace, he noted to his companion, "So many things I have no need for!"

Think about what you *truly* need in order to feel sated, happy, and healthy. The next time you're shopping, consider doing your small part by recalling Socrates's words.

How to Access Strength, Wisdom, and Support with the Visible World

Observe

Spend some time in nature, without the distractions of cell phones, personal music devices, or any kind of technological gadget. Walk on a beach, in a meadow, or along a dirt path near a river. Spend at least an hour noticing your surroundings and how they make you feel. Take a close look at the trees, flowers, and rocks. If you don't know their names, that's okay. Just notice their beauty. Watch the ants collecting crumbs of food to take back to their colonies. Think about how they're working toward the same goals as you are. Every creature tries to both nourish herself and care for the next generation. As you observe the natural world, take pleasure in finding these hidden treasures.

Additionally, get out into an open area at night that's far from the lights of cities at a time when there are no clouds, so you'll have the best view of the stars. See if you notice any constellations, or which ones are the brightest. What is the current phase of the moon? Listen to what creatures make their voices heard at night. Get in touch with how you feel sitting underneath the vast night sky filled with stars and faraway planets. This, if nothing else, will put into perspective the limitless grandeur of the universe in comparison to you, one human creature, who is a minuscule but powerful component of it all.

After you've done what I suggested (or even when you're in the moment), describe your experience in your journal.

Pray

Pray for the world, its oceans and rivers, and its creatures large and small. In praying for your home—this planet—you remind yourself of your connection to it. You remember that it's not a resource to be consumed but a loving mother who provides life and renewal. Say a prayer of thanks for clean air and clean water. Never forget how precious these elements are. Also, pray for those who harm the earth so that they may think before they act, and behave more mercifully.

Act

Our actions have an effect on the larger whole. As you look at the moon or the clouds, vow to live each day embracing wholeliness and noticing the glorious world the Divine has created. Promise to respect everything around you. Make a commitment to living more sustainably with the earth, water, and sky.

Take a moment to look up at the sky. Imagine someone else doing so at the same time and feeling the love you're expressing in the world. Feel a sense of connection to this person who needs your compassion to give him or her strength. See your love filling this individual with courage.

Always be kind to the earth with your actions. Start by changing your behavior in some important way. For instance, buy products that are made closer to your home (which saves fuel). Recycle whatever you can rather than throwing everything away, even if it's somewhat inconvenient to do so. Purchase only ecofriendly or "green" products, or commit to buying them at least some of the time.

Remember that you can always do a little better every day to live in greater harmony with your environment, as we all can; and whatever you're doing for Mother Earth, do more! Change your habits, for every small action on the planet's behalf will help it and all of humanity—and that includes you!

Existing alongside this beautiful, natural visible world is the invisible world. It is also in tune and balanced, and it holds many lessons about wholeliness. When we recognize and value our sacred connections to the invisible world—and understand that in fact, its natural state is wholeliness—our lives change dramatically. This is what I cover in the next chapter.

WHOLELINESS AND THE INVISIBLE WORLD

"People . . . who believe in physics, know that
the distinction between past, present, and future
is only a stubbornly persistent illusion."

— **ALBERT EINSTEIN**

s you reclaim a sense of wholeliness and renew your relationship to the cosmos and the earth, look also at your connections to the invisible world, which exists alongside the visible one.
The invisible realm is where all of us originate, as well as where we
all return after the death of our mortal bodies.

In physics, string theory seems to validate the idea that there
are multiple realities we're unaware of, and this has been ex-
pressed by many great thinkers throughout human history. Jesus
himself said, "In my Father's house are many mansions." Similarly, the *Bhagavata-Purana* states, "Lord Siva said: 'My dear son,
I, Lord Brahma, and the other devas, who rotate within this universe under the misconception of our greatness, can't exhibit any
power to compete with the Supreme Personality of Godhead, for
innumerable universes and their inhabitants come into existence
and are annihilated by the simple direction of the Lord.'" And in
his book *Shaman, Healer, Sage,* Alberto Villoldo, Ph.D., describes

the multiple planes of existence explained to him by his mentor, a Peruvian shaman—he says that the lower planes of existence, such as those of the Stone People and Plant People, have a lower frequency than the higher ones.

The invisible world, with its many planes of existence, is all around us, at all times. This realm is in a different dimension that's beyond the senses. In it, there are no limits of space or time . . . there is only infinite space. There is a boundary between the visible world and the invisible world because the latter is at a higher vibration, but this boundary *can* be crossed.

Spirits who have passed on possess a very high frequency, so it's difficult to perceive them even though they're most definitely involved in your life, watching over you and looking out for your best interests. Some of these spirits don't have a personal connection to you from when they were in physical form, but they're assisting you as part of their attempt to resolve their own karma, which is carried from lifetime to lifetime and from incarnation to incarnation. This relationship is quite harmonious, since helping you offers them opportunities to work through and heal their own wounds from the past, while you receive the gift of assistance from the invisible world.

Life After Death

From the beginning, humans have pondered what happens after we die. Does consciousness continue to exist? Do those who have crossed over continue to interact with us in some way? Or are they removed from our reality, suffering in a place called hell or enjoying peace in a place called heaven?

In cultures all over the world, holy men and women have described an existence beyond suffering. But who is allowed into this heaven or nirvana? Can we all enter freely, or are only those who have lived righteously or hold a particular set of beliefs granted access? What happens to those whose suffering is such that they create bad karma during their time on Earth? What happens to those troubled souls who committed suicide while in the visible world because life was too challenging?

If you think about heaven and hell not as places but as states of being, with the former being a state of higher vibration and the latter being a state of lower vibration, you can get an inkling of how the invisible world works. On the other side, spirits remember the past, because thoughts are a form of energy that can't be destroyed once they've been created, only transformed. In that realm, however, it's not possible to feel sadness, anger, jealousy, or fear. The only emotions that are capable of being experienced are positive ones such as gratitude, joy, and love.

Spirits enjoy their existence in the invisible world. They learn and socialize. They play with their beloved pets, whose souls are there with them as well. They're able to enjoy their favorite foods, even though they don't have bodies and thus don't actually eat. Everything here exists as idea, thought, and memory.

If a person created karma by hurting others when she was in physical form, she becomes very eager to reincarnate in order to work through that issue. This is why spirits in the invisible world will often come through to us with a message of remorse for how they behaved toward us in life. If that spirit was harmed by another, she'll be going through the process of forgiveness, because, as I said, negative emotions can't exist where she is. Spirits want to bring about healing for all. Just as stitches close a wound, an emotional wound closes as well. Our love is what does the healing.

Although we create suffering for ourselves in this life, after we die, it's as if we have a sort of amnesia about how painful it was to be living in our self-created "hell" in the visible world. In fact, ancient Greek texts on the afterlife often portray souls in Hades (the underworld) drinking from the river Lethe so that their physical memories on Earth will be erased and they'll return to corporeal form. Spirits of those who were at a higher consciousness, and therefore created very little karma, might not reincarnate for quite a while, since they feel less of a compulsion to right their wrongs. They may simply choose to stay in the invisible realm and help individuals in the material world create good karma and resolve bad karma.

Those souls who were at a very low consciousness in life reincarnate almost instantly because they have a lot of work to do.

They don't return as the result of a conscious choice, but because of their accumulated karma, that must be resolved. If they "go to hell," that is actually the experience of suffering in this world. Hell does not exist on the other side.

In reality, "The kingdom of heaven is at hand," said Jesus— right alongside us in the invisible world. We experience it whenever we experience joy, love, and compassion. We experience it when we find ourselves in a state of wholeliness.

• • •

Keep in mind that although they can be very busy in the other realm, spirits interact with humans in order to resolve their karma and help bring about wholeliness. All those in the invisible world recognize that there's a Divine plan, but even so, just as they did on Earth, they care about us and thus constructively intervene in our lives in whatever way they can. They're compassionate and want us to learn our lessons through love, not suffering. Our wisest choice is to be open and listen to their guidance.

Spirits don't display bad habits or create karma. They protect people and try to steer wealth, positive people, and good situations toward those they're watching over. Any karmic issues they might have dealt with, such as a habit of being controlling or manipulative, can't affect them in this other realm—and if we have these issues, they want to help us resolve them. Tied to us by love and memory, they make sure to be available for us when we need help.

I had the extraordinary experience of visiting the part of the invisible world where spirits dwell when I nearly drowned in a river at age five. To this day, I can remember incredibly beautiful music resounding as I walked along the lush, green riverbank. I was surrounded by people who were all so peaceful, joyous, and filled with love. They wore simple white garments and communicated without words. I felt so much at home that I was disappointed when I suddenly realized I was being whisked away from this heavenly plane. It was a place of harmony and health, beyond want, need, or scarcity. It was a sacred realm where I felt deeply cared for by all. Everyone there was family. On Earth, we too are all family, but we're blind to that fact because we don't embrace our sacred connections. If we did, this picturesque ideal of heaven could be seen in the visible world.

Messages from Spirit

Our departed loved ones are so much a part of our lives that they will show up as spirits at family parties, Easter mass, and their own funerals. During a recent session for a client named Linda, for instance, her mother came through and told me to relay that she liked the poem her daughter had read at her funeral. This made Linda quite happy, since she'd been worried that it wasn't the right choice.

Next, her mother mentioned that she was learning how to cook in the afterlife, something she'd always meant to do in her physical form. Later, Linda mentioned to me that she thought about what a strange message this was, but then realized that in an earlier version of her remarks at the funeral, she'd intended to make a little joke about her mother's not-so-great cooking because her family had always teased her mother about this. At the last minute, though, Linda had decided to edit this part out. We realized her mother had been acknowledging that she had been present during the planning of the service, and was conveying that she didn't mind being teased. Unlike on our realm, there is no ego or defensiveness on the other side.

In my work, I've seen spirits advising their loved ones to check on specific medical conditions, change travel plans, or stop their secret smoking (yes, they can see you sneak that cigarette!). Sometimes during a session, it may seem as if a spirit is sharing very trivial details. This happens for two reasons: First, it helps the spirit reveal his or her identity, as the details are very often ones that a medium couldn't possibly know. Second, there may be layers to what is being relayed. A spirit who mentions an old acquaintance of yours and says that he's now living in Boston may be letting you know in a subtle way that you will be moving there in the future. Whenever you receive a message, consider all possibilities of what it could mean. Never dismiss the communication as pointless or trivial.

• • •

My daughter and I were relocating from New York to Florida toward the end of December 2009. Perhaps our biggest moving dilemma was how to transfer our three cats and two dogs from one state to the other. I took one cat to Florida via airplane, but that didn't resolve our problem in the least. My daughter was left with the unfortunate duty of having to make the long journey with four animals in her SUV. The most unruly of the bunch was our dog Valentino, an uncannily stubborn Shiba Inu that resembled a fox and refused to take orders from any of us. While they were stopped at a gas station in the rural town of Petersburg, Virginia, Valentino wrangled his head out of his collar and took off into a nearby forest. My daughter spent the next four hours searching for him in the snowy woods in the middle of the night. The next day, she arrived at our home in Florida crying and apologizing for having lost our beloved Valentino.

Although they were very helpful, neither the animal control nor police of Petersburg were able to locate the dog. For three days following the incident, I placed countless ads in the local newspapers and on radio shows. I felt that I needed to find him, and that I shouldn't give up. Valentino was greatly adored by my late husband, and I was confident that his spirit would try to help us in our pursuit. I decided that the only way to get anything done was to go to the site of the incident myself, so I flew up to Virginia on Christmas.

The next two days were spent scouring the neighborhoods and woodland areas of Petersburg, posting flyers on seemingly every lamppost, and screaming "Valentino!" well into the midnight hours as I slowly drove down street after street in my rental car. Every person I approached told me something different: "I saw him ten miles east of here," "He was walking around with a big black dog that way," "He slept in my backyard last night." I collapsed onto the bed in my motel room the second night and thought sadly, *This is hopeless. What a horrible Christmas.* I'd already bought my ticket to return to Florida the following day, so there only remained the small, single, solitary hope that I might find Valentino in the morning before my flight back home. I fell asleep praying to the Divine for a miracle.

My husband came to me in a dream that very night, standing tall and handsome, wearing a brilliant white dress shirt and promising that I would find the dog. "Go toward the place where the dog was lost," he told me. "Get in the car and pay attention to me; I will guide you." I woke up and hopped in the car at the break of dawn. I drove to the gas station where the dog had initially wandered off and parked. I began walking around the area, and then stopped a woman on her way to work.

"Oh, that was your dog?" she responded when asked if she'd spotted him. "Yes, I did, just ten minutes ago. He was sitting right up that way, and the police tried to shoot at him because they thought he was a fox!" she said as she pointed. I thanked the woman and started running in that direction.

Entering the forest, guided totally by pure instinct, I heard my husband say, "Keep going." I made a sudden right and gazed down into a ditch . . . and there was Valentino, keeled over and covered up to his ears in mud, howling feebly for help. I practically tumbled down to him in excitement and hoisted him up in my arms. Had his body not been trembling from the bitter cold, I'm sure he would have jumped at me and licked my face for hours. If he could have spoken, he would have said "Thank you!" a thousand times, but he just stared up at me weakly as I carried him to safety. Truly, this was the best Christmas gift I could have hoped for.

On my way home, I pondered the synchronicities that occurred: Valentino was lost in Virginia and my husband's name was Virgil—all three words begin with the letter *V*. Even more peculiar was the fact that Valentino ran away at 2 A.M. on the 22nd of the month, the exact hour and day my husband had passed away. Ultimately, I believe this was a message about trust: that even when it seems nearly impossible to reconnect with those we love, we must have patience and persevere.

Be Patient and Believe

Spirits long to assist us, but those who have recently crossed over may wait awhile before contacting us or not communicate immediately when we call them. According to some ancient teachings, it's not good to disturb a spirit during the first 40 days after its passing, because it's in a transition period. And indeed, there are those who don't want to do so right after death, perhaps due to this fabled reason. But the day after my father died, I heard him telling me about the letter that he had been writing to me but never got to finish, and the money he had left in his trouser pocket.

I recently did a session for a woman who received contact from her husband who'd died in an accident four weeks before. So it's important to understand there's no general rule about who is and isn't available to talk to us, or when they will. It all depends on the spirit. For example, there may be times when spirits can't come to our assistance because it's too soon after their passing, they're visiting another relative, or they're being called by someone else. But most of the time, they're ready to descend from their ethereal realm when summoned.

When someone you dearly love passes on to the other side, it's devastating. You feel abandoned, as if you've lost a part of your own self. Further, it can be especially difficult to connect with the one you've lost when your heart is in pieces and your mind is swirling with confusion. It becomes even harder to believe that the spirit of that person is around you when you have so much pain inside. But even in your most grief-stricken moments, when it feels impossible to believe that your loved one's spirit is actually with you, *believe*. He will come to you instantly when you call. No matter how much you're hurting, trust that he will come.

Only by believing can you draw the person's energy into your life and truly *feel* its effects. This is the hardest part of the battle, but by understanding that separation from the physical world is not the end of your loved one's soul, and certainly not the end of your relationship, you *can* overcome the disbelief. This is the key to carrying on with your life after you've been devastated by the loss of someone very dear to your heart. Then, after you've initially made contact with him, continue to do so. Speak to him as if he were still here with you, right in your home.

• • •

It's very common for spirits to come through in a dream. One of my clients named Cecile told me that her mother came to her in this way via an answering-machine message. This was especially powerful because Cecile had asked her mother for some reassurance that she was handling a certain situation properly that concerned both of them. Her mother's recording, in the dream, included a wish for a happy Mother's Day (which was actually many months off). Although the message was not direct, but symbolic, Cecile understood. She told me that during the dream, she was aware that this was very real and not just her imagination. When *you* dream of someone who has died, and sense that it's real, know that it truly is. That spirit is communicating, so pay attention.

Loved ones who have passed on can also leave hints that they're with you. Perhaps you'll do a double-take when you glance at a man walking his dog and swear that he's your late brother. You might notice your spouse's name spoken randomly on TV, or printed on a truck or a sign. You may dream about your grandmother doing an ordinary activity that she used to do with you, such as telling you a story by the fire or preparing a meal. Or perhaps you'll note that something has moved inexplicably from one room of your house to another, or that the lights are on when you return home even though you clearly remember having turned them off. Don't disregard these signs: they're all clear symbols from the ones who continue to love you despite their passing. When they occur, stop what you're doing, become quiet, and concentrate on this person. Notice whether you feel his or her presence.

Spirits usually communicate in an energetic form, entering your thoughts and dreams. But if you're fortunate and very open, you may sense that your loved one is actually touching or holding you. This is a powerful experience, and one you can pray for—but you must also accept that it doesn't always happen.

Sometimes people come to me asking for specific information from a spirit. They want to know the location of a lost item (such as an insurance policy or will), or how their loved one died. If the person was murdered—or there's some question as to whether the death was the result of a homicide, suicide, or accident—the client may be very eager to get a specific answer. Keep in mind that spirits, who don't experience lower emotions, have different priorities than we do. Their primary concern is healing of themselves and others. And as I've said, they're very aware that there's a Divine plan. If they choose not to reveal information to the living, they have good reason, and we must accept that. We too will come to understand their reasons in the future.

Having said that, do feel free to ask for signs that will reassure you of their presence: Ask them for guidance out loud. Leave them a glass of water, wine, or their favorite drink at their preferred seat at the table as a means of inviting them to visit you. Your loved one is with you and will try to communicate if you're open to the messages.

If you suddenly think about this individual in an odd moment, quiet your mind and open your heart to feeling his spirit's presence. Say to him: "I love you still, and I miss you." It's okay to cry when this happens. You can use the opportunity to release your negative emotions. The boundary between our realm and the one inhabited by those who have passed is real, even if it's thin, and it's very hard for us to accept that our relationship with that person has changed.

I speak from personal experience on this. Since I'm advanced in the communication abilities of the mind, I'm very open to my late husband visiting me, which he often does. But it's not the same as when we used to share meals, drive to the beach, and so on. Like anyone, I cry and mourn my loss. Even so, I try to remain open so that I can cherish each moments that he's with me.

• • •

After a loved one from the invisible world comes through in a dream or you've been given a clear sign that she was in your home, you'll feel relief and an emotional upsurge. With courage and an open heart, overcome your fear of a visitor from the other realm and accept her attempts to contact you.

Many people are scared of spirits because of how our society has portrayed them. They think that "ghosts" are these terribly frightening things that go bump in the night and do everything they can to scare the life out of those of us on Earth. In reality, they've been portrayed this way in TV and film in order to generate money, since it's not as exciting to watch a friendly ghost coming to visit.

But such is not the case when communicating with those spirits whom you were close to when they were in the physical realm: remember that they don't want to frighten you; they only want you to acknowledge their presence. The more you allow them into your heart and thoughts, the more you will be guided in your problems, concerns, and issues. As you open yourself to receiving messages from those who are no longer with you, the healing process will become easier.

Since they understand that we're not always ready for their messages, spirits know it's good to plant seeds to prepare us for unexpected or unpleasant events. For example, during my father's funeral, I suddenly began to hear his voice: "Look behind my grave and remember the name on the tombstone. When you arrive in America, you will meet a man by that name. He will be very important to you. He will change your life." When I peeked behind my father's grave, I noticed that the plot was, according to the headstone, reserved for a man named Virgil. Thanks to this clue, I had someone quite specific to look forward to meeting who would bring me great happiness.

A few days after my initial arrival in New York City, I was scheduled to sing at a concert hall. After the show finished, a very handsome and charming man came over to greet me. He held out his hand . . . and introduced himself as Virgil. Needless to say, I almost fell over in shock! And in a matter of weeks, I married him (clearly, he was my soul mate)! We lived together happily for 27 years until he passed away.

Unfortunately, the fact that I first learned my husband's name from a tombstone also served to foreshadow his premature death. Many years later, right after he passed away, I returned to visit my father's grave in Romania and noticed that the site that had first revealed the name Virgil had been filled.

• • •

The invisible and visible worlds both operate similarly. If you can let go of your ego's false belief that death is the end of your individual consciousness, you will find it easier to perceive the incredible connections you can have with those who have died. You'll be more open to their messages and lessons for you. Then you can make wiser, more carefully guided decisions in life, thus suffering through fewer mistakes. With access to the other realm, power, peace, and healing will be yours to enjoy.

How to Communicate with the Invisible World

Observe

You may have already interacted with a spirit, but you dismissed the experience because it was frightening or confusing or you thought you were imagining things at the time. If so, write about what happened. Try to put aside your mental fear of a visitor from beyond: remember that there is nothing to be alarmed about, and attempt to overcome the false stereotypes that TV and film have associated with ghosts. Talk about this topic with someone you can trust and who is also a believer.

Remember that by observing and acknowledging the presence of spirits in our lives, we let them know we're open to their guidance and messages.

Pray

Of course, it's important to pray to the Divine for guidance—but you may also pray to your guardian angels, the saints, or to those who have passed into the invisible world. Ask to feel a connection to them, along with signs that they're working on your behalf. They will happily work to satisfy these requests. For example, one of my clients prayed to her grandmother, who always helped her out financially, and the next day discovered a stash of silver dollars that Grandma had left behind in a jewelry box. Although the coins weren't worth all that much, this was a way her spirit was communicating to help her granddaughter resolve her difficult situation.

I seek Divine guidance from absolutely everyone on the other side: God, Jesus, saints, family members . . . whoever is listening! Every one of them helps me in a different way: I pray to my father for financial advice, to my mother for emotional stability, to Spirit to express gratitude for what I have, to St. Anthony for help in finding misplaced items, and so on. You may want to request something specific from your loved ones as well.

Act

If you haven't seen a medium work, have a session with one or watch one do a reading. Seek out one who can assist you in feeling that you're making contact and validate that you're receiving guidance from the other side. This will awaken you to the reality of your interconnectedness with the invisible world. Instead of merely believing that spirits exist, you may find that it's more accurate to say you've *experienced* that they are among us.

To have contact with those on the other side through so-called paranormal phenomena is to recognize that you're directly connected to the Divine *and* to spirits working on your behalf. Don't be scared of making this connection! Trouble-seeking spirits may exist, but they're very weak and won't interact with you unless you're in a very dark, negative state. Even then they won't harm you; they'll just depress you further. By calling upon Spirit and those who have passed over, you won't have to worry about attracting any of these unwanted energies that might lower your vibration and upset you.

If you acknowledge your sacred, healing connections with spirits in the invisible realm, you will become more courageous and find yourself able to face up to any negativity that you've caused. No one is free from sin, as Jesus said; indeed, none of us goes through life without at times violating the moral rule of being good and loving others. Yet you can make up for your errors and heal the wounds you've created in yourself and others. In fact, even though it's a commonly misunderstood process, healing karma is possible simply by embracing wholeliness, as you'll find out next.

WHOLELINESS
AND KARMA

"That each, who seems a separate whole,
Should move his rounds, and fusing all
The skirts of self again, should fall,
Remerging in the general soul . . ."

— ALFRED, LORD TENNYSON

Westerners don't tend to be as familiar with the concept of karma as people in the East are, so there's much confusion about what, exactly, karma is and how it works. It's not the universe's way of punishing us for doing wrong, or simply "what goes around comes around"—*it's the natural result of our actions.* In fact, the term *karma* is a Sanskrit word that means "the force generated by a person's actions." The law of karma is one of my Eleven Eternal Principles, and it can be summed up this way: what we do and what happens to us are the results of our souls' choice to come to Earth to learn the lessons we need to learn.

You may find it helpful to think of karma as the soul's memory. Negative memories create emotional wounds you must mend and psychological issues you must resolve. Positive memories, or "good karma," can balance out negative memories, helping you heal and move closer to the harmony of wholeness. And just as there is personal ego and group ego, there is personal karma and group karma—so you may be emotionally wounded as a consequence of the actions others take. If you *are* suffering as a result of what others do, you're certainly not to blame for group karma.

In fact, let go of the idea of blame altogether. Karma is not concerned with who's at fault; it's about healing wounds, and the only way to do so is by healing the emotions that those wounds generate. When you work on your karma, you don't forget that someone once hurt you, but you do let go of the dark emotions that were attached to the memory of that event *and* stop creating more of them whenever you think about it. The energetic vibration of anger, hatred, or sadness is very low and will clog your chakras (but automatically clears when you die and cross over into the invisible realm).

You may have experienced this when you were reminded of something bad that happened to you that you hadn't thought about in a long time. As I said, in the invisible world, those who have passed retain their memories, but they don't hang on to the painful emotions they had on Earth. In the visible world, these feelings often become a part of us, so it can be very difficult to let them go.

Strong emotions arise whenever we think about the lover who cheated on us or the parent who harshly criticized us. As a result, we give these feelings more power, which allows them to generate more anguish. We find ourselves thinking, *That's right, I forgot how painful it was when he left me. Why haven't I gotten over him? What's wrong with me? I'm so mad at myself. I thought I healed that old wound!* We then continue to have the same reaction of negativity whenever we encounter a situation similar to the old one that originally hurt us. And while we try to avoid thinking about those painful memories, too often we wallow in our darker emotions and reinforce them. Ultimately, this prevents us from achieving healing.

Each time the karmic wheel turns and the same situations and emotions come back into our lives, we have a choice. Do we respond in the same old way, or do we break the habit and free ourselves? Although each of us will experience negative karma in one way or another throughout life, this doesn't have to scar us or throw us into a cycle of repetitive behavior. We can make tremendous progress toward resolving our karma if we understand how it works, love ourselves and others enough to practice forgiveness as a way of life, and always act upon the principles of wholeliness.

"Why Is This Happening to Me?"

After telling me their woes, many of the people I've counseled over the years have asked, "Why is this terrible thing happening to me?" They're not experiencing bad luck or God's punishment for something they've done, but they somehow fell victim to the inevitable turn of the wheel of fortune, also known as the wheel of karma.

Reincarnation is the transmigration of the soul from one body to another after death. So the fact that our souls carry with them the unresolved karma from our previous lives into this one explains why we not only suffer the consequences of our actions in life, but also why situations that seem so unjust occur as well. Babies who die young, children who are stricken with terrible diseases or born into abusive families, and good people who meet tragic ends all may be working through the consequences of karma from a past life.

Even in the New Testament we find evidence for reincarnation. Jesus's disciples asked him if a blind man who had sinned should have to suffer from this condition—was it the man who had sinned or his parents? Jesus responded: "Neither this man nor his parents sinned, but this happened so that the works of God might be displayed in him" (John 9:2–3). Jesus also said that John the Baptist was the reincarnation of Elijah: "And if you are willing to accept it, John himself is Elijah who was to come" (Matthew 11:14).

As I briefly mentioned earlier, karma that affects someone who seems to be having bad luck may have been created by the group he belongs to, such as his family or community. In the West, we focus so much on individuality that it's hard for us to remember that wholeliness applies here, too. Because we're all connected to one another, if someone next to us is hurt, we become hurt as well.

If we witness a tragedy, our natural empathy for a fellow human being causes us to be traumatized even though we aren't the one who was killed, abused, or sick. Further, while a soldier may himself escape death or injury in war, he often returns home haunted by having seen others suffer—and if he doesn't resolve this karma, it will affect him in the future. In this way, the anguish of others greatly impacts us.

Knowing how interconnected we all are, and that we suffer each other's pain, helps us see that karma isn't meant to punish us. The Divine doesn't intend for a good soldier protecting his people to be punished, or for a child to have a congenital physical ailment. Tragedies and suffering happen because of the karma that follows us from incarnation to incarnation, unless we recognize its need to be repaired and finally heal it.

• • •

None of us can know all of our karmic influences. So rather than wonder how you might have caused an event, it's better to ponder, *What can I learn from this experience? How can I use it as an opportunity for growth, for resolving my karma, and for contributing to the healing and well-being of all?* These are all empowering questions, because exploring their answers will lead to healing. Eventually they will put your traumas into perspective and allow you to regain harmony and balance in your life.

In psychology, the tendency to repeat the same negative behaviors is called the "repetition compulsion." In other words, if you only address them cognitively, you won't move past them. You can vow to change, only to be frustrated and bewildered when you fall back into the same old patterns after you thought you'd overcome your habit. The solution is to address the upsetting memory that led to your creating more bad karma.

Your soul is drawn toward opportunities for facing your issues; acknowledging them; forgiving yourself for any part you've played in creating them; and letting go of the feelings of sorrow, anger, or fear that are woven into the memory. If you resist using the opportunity to heal, you perpetuate imbalance and disharmony.

That's why you sometimes attract into your life events that make you fearful, situations that cause you pain, and people who hurt you—you're meant to recognize these circumstances as karmic and resolve them once and for all.

As uncomfortable as it may be to revisit an old wound, you absolutely must. *Unless you deliberately process your unresolved karmic issues, they'll trap you in a cycle of repetitive behavior.* And the more you engage in self-hatred for what you've done in the past, the more you're trapped. Self-loathing worsens your suffering and deepens the wounds that are already so painful; thus, you end up burying memories and refusing to look at them again.

Note that you should never look to alcohol or drugs to blot out memories of old wounds, as these substances are no substitute for Divine help. Instead, call upon Spirit for courage, hope, and love. With strength received from Source, you'll be able to acknowledge what you've done—no matter how ugly the behavior—and use your conscious mind to choose forgiveness.

Forgiveness doesn't mean forgetting what happened and denying your pain. It means *letting go* of your negative feelings instead of keeping them bottled up inside. Then you can look honestly at the experience and learn your lessons so that you can avoid similar situations in the future.

Even if the other people involved have shown no remorse, forgive them because it will free you from more suffering. Loving yourself and others means that you make better choices, so you don't go on to create more pain for yourself or others. It also means helping the other individuals come back to a state of wholeliness. Instead of wishing for them to experience negative emotions, wish that they might feel remorse and atone so that they can heal from the karma they've generated.

Embracing the Totality of a Person

All of us have a dark side, as well as distressing memories of having behaved badly. Because it's extremely uncomfortable to admit this, we'd rather point a finger at someone else whose dark side has been revealed and think, *At least I'm not as bad as he is.* After all, it's human nature to demonize others for their failings and overlook our own.

Yet no one is all bad or all good. We're the totality of all our qualities, and we have both subconscious and conscious impulses. A man might think that he wants monogamy and emotional intimacy with his spouse—and was even fully committed to his marriage when he said his vows—but because of his unresolved karma, he may not live up to this. Perhaps he feels undeserving of happiness, or is terrified of having emotional and sexual intimacy with the same person. Maybe he's insecure and drawn to seducing other women in order to address those feelings, only to find himself dealing with extreme guilt after he's betrayed his wife. Because his karma is unresolved, this behavior creates more bad karma.

While we can easily condemn this man's behavior, it's not right to deem him a bad person. He might not seem to be suffering because of his ability to deny the emotional impact of his actions, but his soul knows that there's tremendous disharmony in his energy field. It's also possible that he may well manifest physical illness as a result of the disorder in his soul.

To resolve karma and return to wholeliness, stop seeing yourself and others as all good or all bad, as victims or victimizers. You must acknowledge the totality of everyone, the complexity and contradictions in each behavior. The most loving person can be harsh and judgmental when she's under strain, while the most self-centered person can become rather generous in a crisis where he's presented with the opportunity to help another. Also know that you can't simply peer into someone and see all of her hidden wounds. In fact, she might not even be aware of them herself! You simply have to trust that bad behavior comes from earlier emotional damages and a feeling of disconnection. By embracing wholeliness, you will help others heal and feel connected—and stop creating so much bad karma.

Keep in mind that the ego enjoys the illusion of control and wisdom that comes from thinking you truly know those who you're close to and can predict their behaviors. So when a gentle and easygoing friend suddenly snaps after months or years of stress and commits a terrible act, it's very unsettling. Such events are reminders that everyone has a dark side, and people aren't always who they seem to be on the surface. And while some may have more karma to resolve than you do, that shouldn't be your concern. You're not here to "fix" anyone else, or to make comparisons and judgments. When you do that, it's because your ego wants to avoid doing the work of resolving your own karma!

Again and again, this misplaced focus occurs in our celebrity-driven culture. We love to gossip when a famous person is revealed to have done something wrong because it deflects our attention away from our own issues. Celebrities themselves feel the pressure to be perfect—to always have a smile on their faces and be polite, understanding, and patient to everyone at all times. Our insistence that someone in the public eye must always appear delightful is a huge burden on him.

Many people from other walks of life take on such a burden as well, feeling that they have to live up to unrealistic expectations. The need to please everyone can drive such individuals to anxiety and depression. It's exhausting to have to constantly satisfy others but never be allowed to satisfy themselves. All human beings need to feel that they can express unhappiness and anger without being rejected by, or disconnected from, those they love. In fact, those who haven't worked through their issues, and find themselves always letting down those they care about, are often extremely lonely. They feel unloved and unlovable because they're not seeing their totality. They're not acknowledging all the aspects of themselves, which is the first step in resolving karma.

● ● ●

To bury *any* side of yourself—your dark side, your compassionate side, your creative side, or whatever it is—is to contradict wholeliness and create disharmony. If you love yourself, it's easier to find the strength to look at your failings, accept them, and address them.

Spirit and spirits are always there to help you with this diffi-cult process of accepting your own totality, as well as that of oth-ers. Although it may seem as if guides, angels, and spirits are not there when you're going through trauma and turbulence, that's only because they have to act in alignment with the law of karma and not prevent you from learning crucial lessons. They'd rather you figure things out in a less painful way, but like everyone, you may have to suffer to awaken to your karma. The priority of spirits is the healing of all, not the prevention of pain in an individual. But that, too, will come after your soul is healed.

In fact, the priority of Spirit, and all the souls within the col-lective consciousness, is to resolve the karma of humanity and bring everyone back to wholeliness. The Divine's wisdom stretch-es beyond human understanding. You might see the loss of a house or job as a terrible stroke of luck, but later you recognize that without this experience, you wouldn't have ended up in a much better place. So just remember: if something doesn't work out, something better surely awaits.

The Power of Group Karma

Exacting revenge and punishing those who have harmed us are very human responses to the pain of facing our karma. These reactions stem from our disconnection from wholeliness, and thus from our inability to forgive and more forward . . . and they simply result in creating more negative karma. We can't get out of this endless cycle by lashing out against others or giving in to distrust and suspicion. When we create the illusion of separation between our group and another, we perpetuate bad karma instead of healing it. We see this with bigotry and racism. Today, many of us are continuing to perpetuate the ancient judgments that lighter-skinned people are better than darker-skinned people—even when we know this behavior, which goes back hundreds or thousands of years, is so wrong. For example, in India, where the wealthier Brahmin class has lighter skin than the poorer "untouchable" class, we see the same divisions and bigotry as we do in America, where the legacy of slavery can still be felt today.

The only way to break this behavior that continues to plague us is to embrace wholeliness and show love to all. You may be Canadian, for instance, while I'm European, but on a larger scale, we're both inhabitants of planet Earth. You may be homosexual and I heterosexual, but don't we both seek love and acceptance from a partner? You may be agnostic where I believe in God, but aren't we both searching for answers and a sense of being connected to something larger than ourselves that sustains us and gives our lives meaning? Regardless of our creed, race, sexual orientation, or history, our paths are all interconnected. It's time we get past our differences and focus on our unity.

During the American Civil War, Abraham Lincoln quoted the Bible when he warned: "A house divided against itself cannot stand." He knew that empires crumble as a result of internal strife. As their very union was faced with tremendous challenges, Lincoln asked Americans to come together instead of squaring off against each other.

In the United States today, people sense that the empire we've all taken for granted for so long is on a shaky foundation because too many of us have become greedy and fearful. While our daily lives are being interrupted by natural disasters, a housing crisis that will take years to come out of, and financial troubles that no one knows how to fix, we treat the symptoms and not the source: the sense of disconnection that causes us to create and perpetuate bad karma.

Recently, I've heard several stories from my clients and friends who are shocked by the aggressive and unethical behavior of private and government debt collectors. I've tried to reassure them by pointing out that when human beings are afraid, we go after each other aggressively. Most of us hate feeling that we're being unfair or not playing by the rules, but when we're scared, we begin to think: *It's me against the world.* Consideration for anyone else flies out the window. Yet this madness has to stop.

At some point, those who are participating in corruption and abuse need to stand with those who are being wrongly persecuted to reject the idea that in order to secure their own safety, they have to do wrong by their neighbor. There's no safety in being a part of the group that holds on to power at any cost without concern for others. In the end, they'll be turned on as well!

Let's look at what can happen when a government mis handles its authority by recalling the Roman Empire. You see, Rome tried to secure its power by conquering and exploiting civilizations in other lands, only to have barbarians begin to fight back. The Roman emperor Diocletian raised taxes to a ridiculous degree to compensate for the government running out of money. The government was stretched so far that it became virtually impossible to maintain control, especially when officials were constantly bickering and people who'd been forced into becoming Roman resisted assimilation and refused to share or respect the values of their new country. Yet despite all the signs that disharmony was going to bring the empire to its knees, the proud people of Rome thought that they were invincible and believed that what they'd created would last forever. Does this sound familiar? America needs to more deeply ponder its national and international problems—after all, any sovereignty, government, or institution can fall apart.

Then there's Atlantis. Whether or not this society truly existed or was a fable, it has captured the imagination of many over the course of Western civilization because it's undeniably reflective of what happens to an empire that crumbles from within. According to Plato's account, Atlantis was technologically advanced, but began warring with others, including the darker-skinned Lemurians. The bad karma of the people of Atlantis, combined with their greed and cruelty, caused the island to sink into the ocean.

Perhaps the legend of Atlantis will hit home in America, which has yet to curb its bigotry, greed, and aggressiveness. We all have to pay for the sins of our fathers, because, according to the Law of Totality, we *are* our fathers. Ultimately, we cannot continue to run from what we need to resolve, no matter how many centuries have passed or how many empires have come and gone. Bad karma doesn't disappear just because a person or group dies.

America has the potential to be a role model for the world. It's had many shining moments in history: when we've lived up to the ideals set forth by our Founding Fathers and other patriots who had a deep appreciation for wholeliness. At present, we have the choice to turn back to unifying, inspiring values or fall deeper into conflict, suspicion, bigotry, and a lust for power. The decline can be stopped, but only if harmony is brought back to the fore. But when the top 2 percent of the population controls most of the wealth and millions struggle to afford the basic securities of liberty, our nation will continue to be unstable.

• • •

Every day, thousands of individuals are creating good karma and doing their best to improve the systems we've designed: for instance, young people who have been shut out of the traditional pathways to security are envisioning and creating new ways of living and working. Only positive outcomes will result from questioning our systems and materialistic ways that aren't making anyone happy. And improvements will start from the smallest changes. For example, people with basements, attics, and garages full of cheap goods (some with tags still on them) will realize that all their "stuff" isn't making them feel any better; in fact, it's causing them to feel trapped. If we all made an effort to live more simply and downsize, we'd notice a positive difference in society.

Have you gotten caught in the clutches of materialism? Have you felt pressured to buy, own, and collect more? If so, then without realizing it, you may have started becoming totally focused on things and forgotten how much more joy and security you feel when you simply invest in your relationships with yourself, others, and Spirit. There's no reason to feel ashamed if you've gotten swept away by the desire for possessions. Forgive yourself and vow to live differently now that you're aware of just how fully you turned toward the illusion that you can buy happiness.

Globally, an economic crisis was essential in order to bring the human race back to wholeliness. Nowadays, people everywhere are realizing they don't want to have prosperity at the expense of the poor feeling no sense of safety or hope for improving their situation. We can all enjoy the bounty of the earth if we choose to share and live sustainably, frugally, and harmoniously. We have the ability to create good karma and resolve the issues that continually manifest more negativity. I believe that men, women, and children everywhere are integrating these more modest behaviors into their lives; in the future, we will see this continue to increase, as more of us awaken to wholeliness.

We're Not Here to Be Rescued

The desire for someone to rescue us by giving us instant fixes is understandable, but the reality is that we all have to work to resolve our karma. We can't keep looking to leaders to save us. While those who are in control may have every intention of helping, they're ultimately limited in their power, while corruption is a greater temptress to them than to ordinary people. We mistakenly see them as omnipotent, and become angry and vilify them when they don't meet our expectations. We need to appreciate the good a leader is able to accomplish and stop holding him or her to such high standards. After all, we're not meant to look outside of ourselves for healing, but within.

Too many of us haven't experienced the process of healing our own karma, so we have little faith in ourselves and our ability to solve our own problems. I've counseled many divorced people over the years, and lots of them are still bitter about the past. Unfortunately, their distrust and cynicism colors their perception whenever they meet someone new. They think that they can be rescued from their loneliness by a perfect soul mate, but they aren't open to hearing that this perception will hold them back from the love they're seeking. I tell them, "Vital to your happiness is realizing that you must be the one to rescue yourself from loneliness."

Some of my divorced clients have taken my words to heart— they've had the courage to explore their roles in relationships and envision how they might act differently the next time in order to create harmony between them and their new partner. The ones who make the most progress are those who are willing to go back as far as necessary into their own past to heal old issues. They forgive their parents for being imperfect, and themselves for not knowing any better than they did. Love allows them to transcend the bitterness and pain and to learn what they need in order to have a healthier relationship the next time. Love ultimately allows them to let go of the fantasy of rescue and resolve their own karma.

Our societies, governments, corporations, and institutions need to take the same approach. Looking for a bailout or a hero to save them will not work. Everyone involved has to find the courage to face their karma and work through it instead of deny it and blame their problems on others.

Intention springs from the courage and creativity to dream of a better tomorrow. However, it's not enough to intend to bring about a new system, relationship, or world; intention alone doesn't resolve the karma that holds you back. That is, healing doesn't happen in the material realm when it remains a mere thought stuck in your mind. *You must act.*

The Divine is there to help you, but it won't rush in and rescue you as if you were a helpless infant. By allowing you to experience suffering, Spirit intends for you to recognize the importance of working through your karma and developing a higher level of consciousness, one that is loving and compassionate toward yourself and others. The Divine wants you to look to other people for assistance, too. But it's your job to make a conscious choice to embrace wholeliness over separateness, and to heal yourself instead of concentrating on revenge and harming others.

Perhaps you're ambivalent about your karma because deep down you want to avoid suffering and you think it would be easier to ignore your pain and cover it up with positive thoughts. This is a form of denial, and it won't work. Healing doesn't happen automatically, but it does happen more easily when you trust in wholeliness.

To resolve karma, you need to make a choice to catch yourself each time you're behaving out of alignment with Divine law and adjust your behavior by substituting new, healthier behaviors. And be patient, because this undoubtedly takes practice. Start by making this observation, connect to the love and compassion of Spirit in order to feel supported, and then take action.

As you tackle your own issues, you'll make progress toward dissolving the karma we all share and contribute to global healing.

How to Help Heal the Karma of the World

Not many cultures encourage people to investigate their individual or collective problems. In the West, for instance, we focus quite a bit on superficial matters. We're inundated with advertisements and media messages that encourage self-centeredness, and jingoism—the belief that "my group is better than yours"—is embraced by far too many. The lack of support for introspection and atonement causes us to have great difficulty admitting that we actually did something wrong and contributed to the creation of harm for others.

When we do create bad karma as individuals or as societies, we're likely to just skip over it rather than examine what we might learn from the situation. We say we don't want to get caught in the "blame game" or dwell on the past, but we're often quick to pick ourselves up and begin sprinting forward without so much as a thought about what the lesson of that experience was. Whether it's the divorced person blaming the failure of the marriage on "that awful partner of mine," or a country blaming global problems on other countries, it's human nature to avoid addressing painful karmic issues.

As individuals and members of a larger whole, we must slow down and admit our failings, analyze their causes, and heal our wounds by applying self-awareness and courage. A "can do" spirit of reinvention has its merits, but it must be balanced by analyzing what we've done and truly learning from past mistakes. Only then can we evolve and come closer to manifesting wholeliness.

To achieve greater balance and avoid the trap of letting go of the past before we've learned from it, we must resist any denial of failure. We should think as individuals, but act for the good of the whole. We have to heal our own inner wounds, but also those we inflicted on others and those the larger group we belong to has created. But we can only make a difference when we remember our sacred connections and embrace the totality of who we all are: light and dark, and good and bad.

• • •

Although the world shares karma, you can't be the one to resolve it simply because you want to do good. You can try to help, but you can't fix the planet all by yourself. So let your anger or sorrow arise, but then let it fade. Draw strength from your sacred connections and the love, hope, and courage they provide.

The good you create heals the bad, but not necessarily in real time; that is, you may not actually see the direct effects. It's not that your actions were inconsequential, but that the workings of karma are complex. Your positive energy could have affected something other than what you intended to influence, and you may never know it. The important thing is that it did make a difference.

You may have to let go of your strong need to "fix" one specific person or bring a certain group to a higher level of consciousness. Perhaps you can't convince your friends, family members, or co-workers to change their behavior. Trust in wholeliness anyway, because you just never know who is watching or gaining inspiration from your compassionate actions. Besides, acting from love will give you the courage to let go of your obligation to fix others and assist you in gravitating toward and attracting those who are at a higher level of consciousness. You can then support each other because you're on the same karmic level.

Two very helpful techniques for discovering hidden karma are dream analysis and hypnosis. Dreaming brings memories or problems stored away in your conscious awareness to the surface, and you may also encounter the spirits who wish to communicate messages to you. Whenever you have a dream or nightmare that makes a strong impression upon you or is repeated, pay attention. Look at what the symbols might represent. If you're in therapy, it's important to tell your therapist if you've had a powerful or recurring dream. Therapy supports you in healing karma, and it will often bring up thoughts that were buried in your subconscious mind, because you're now able to handle that information.

Hypnosis is a more direct way of accessing dormant memories. It's a reconstruction of sleep, and a trained psychologist can extract just the right information from your subconscious. Once recovered, these images can help you make tremendous progress that would have otherwise required much more effort. As I mentioned in the Preface, I earned a Ph.D. in hypnotherapy because I recognized what an incredible tool it is, and I wanted to help my patients move forward quickly into healing!

Several years ago, I had a client named Marcus who needed to do a lot of traveling for his job. He came to me to resolve his fear of flying, since it was hampering his ability to achieve his professional goals. It was also costing him money because he would buy airplane tickets, become anxious and scared, and be unable to board his flight due to panic. He was self-aware enough to recognize that he had a pattern of avoidance. But knowing that he needed to change—and genuinely wanting to do so—wasn't enough. He needed help in overcoming his phobia.

We began our first hypnosis session that day, and almost immediately I was able to draw out of him a memory of being the pilot of a plane that crashed into the Atlantic Ocean and killed everyone on board. After reassuring Marcus that it was safe for him to explore the emotions attached to this event, I brought him back to a fully conscious state. He remembered the session and was amazed by what his subconscious mind had revealed: a traumatic experience from a past life that explained his irrational fear of flying. We did a few more sessions together so that he could rid himself of his negative associations with flying and replace them with positive ones.

The next time Marcus flew, he informed me that he'd suffered the usual panic attacks for the first several minutes, but then inexplicably felt much calmer. This gave him the courage to try again, and the second time he flew he was somewhat uncomfortable, but better able to tolerate his nervousness.

Using dream analysis or hypnosis can help you cure phobias, obsessive patterns, addictions, and mood disorders, all of which are rooted in karma. It becomes much easier to revisit uncomfortable situations through hypnosis than if you were to simply will yourself to do so consciously. Ideally, you should work with a therapist who is accepting and nonjudgmental so that you can trust that you'll be totally supported as you uncover painful memories.

How to Heal Your Karma

Observe

Pay attention to your dreams and their messages, as well as images or thoughts that often come to you or seem to show up in your life. Your dreams or nightmares can be a reflection of the negative karma that raps at the door of your subconscious mind, so ponder their significance. Don't forget to ask for guidance from the Divine and the spirits who are supporting you—they'll give you the wisdom and courage to decipher these messages and accept what you've learned, painful though this process may be.

Observe the connections between your past and present. What themes seem to keep coming up in your life? Do you find yourself mirroring the behavior of people who harmed you in the past? Do you find yourself in the same old self-defeating patterns?

If you feel emotions that are out of proportion with a situation, don't chide yourself for being overly sensitive. Use it as an opportunity to explore your karma. Try to pinpoint what it is from your past that's causing you to respond sensitively to certain things. If you're upset by a news story, figure out what part of it is most upsetting to you. Does it remind you of something from your past? What issues have you left unresolved? Write down your reflections in your journal.

Pray

Request that the Divine help you discover your karma and heal it. Ask for assistance in finding the courage to face your karma and resolve it so that you don't continue to suffer or hurt others. Pray that facing your negative karma will not be emotionally painful.

Ask Spirit to show you how to heal the karma of your group, whether it's your family, your ethnic or religious group, or your country. Acknowledge your wrongdoings together rather than focusing on how you personally didn't participate in those behaviors. Pray to be healed of any tendency to act negatively. Petition for the strength to stand up for those who aren't part of your group, to be a brave soul who works to heal karma and create good in the world. Ask for healing of the whole.

Act

If you're feeling stuck in destructive behavior patterns, whether that means avoiding intimacy with others or taking part in addictive behaviors, please consider consulting a therapist and working with hypnosis to get to the root of your karma. Hypnosis can help you shed the surface layers of your conscious mind in order to access the subconscious and reach the root of a problem.

If you feel that you're aware of your karmic or psychological issues, write out a description of how you'd like to change and what qualities you wish to embody. Create a vision for yourself as a healed person who is free of negative karma. Just as every sports team devises a plan before a game starts, spell out how you're going to change yourself for the better. Actually imagine how you'll behave in specific situations that tend to trigger your anger or frustration.

Know ahead of time how you want to respond before you're confronted with gossip, cheaters, and victimizers so that you can make different choices. Prepare yourself for moments that will test you. Imagine who you might become—then write out this vision for yourself and revisit it often, affirming the person that you're becoming.

Never doubt that you *can* be the person you want to be. Every small act of courage counts. Your day to change is today; it is as perfect a day to begin healing as any other. Chances are that if you set forth the intention to heal, the universe will respond almost instantly with an opportunity to follow through on that commitment.

Negative karma prevents you from being whole and healed. It's like having an open wound in your spirit. This wound, deepened whenever you give in to destructive thoughts or emotions, can actually materialize as illness. The manifestation of emotions as physical ailments is not meant to punish you but to awaken you to your unresolved karma and your need to return to a state of wholeliness.

·· ● ··

WHOLELINESS AND THE BODY, MIND, AND SPIRIT

*"You have metabolized your past
and given it sanctuary in your body.
Or as someone put it simply,
'The issues are in the tissues.'"*

— DEEPAK CHOPRA

A
s I've said before, our natural state is wholeliness: the experience of physical, mental, and spiritual well-being and health. We were designed to be disease free, healthy, and whole. The body, mind, and spirit are meant to be in balance with each other. Too much focus on thoughts and emotions, or too much attention paid to the body, creates an imbalance—as does a quest for spirituality at the expense of physical needs. When body, mind, and spirit are all equally attended to, there is peace and contentment. When all three levels of the self are in harmony, we wake up every day loving the gift of life a little more.

A lifestyle that promotes wellness on all levels will reduce the risk of illness and imbalance. Physical vitality, mental clarity, and spiritual tranquility combined are what we should strive for to ensure a longer life. Exercising daily, having a strong relationship with the Divine, consuming whole and organic foods, reducing stress levels, avoiding addictive substances, enjoying positive relationships, and following the wisdom of our greatest teachers are the best ways to bring about health at all levels.

The Interconnectedness of Health

You probably weren't taught to notice the connections between your own well-being and that of others. Yet it can be very enlightening to step back and look at how being a part of a larger group that's not fostering wellness affects you—as well as how your imbalanced mind, body, or spirit influences others. Are all of your peers on antidepressants and stressed-out by the demands of their lifestyle? Are many of your neighbors, friends, or family members struggling with prediabetic or diabetic conditions while they continue to urge you to eat sugary treats? When you don't take care of your emotions and find yourself so overloaded that you develop a cold or the flu, do you notice a shift in the behavior of those you interact with?

You may be under pressure to ignore the signs that are telling you to bring your whole self back into balance, because taking time out to do so might inconvenience others. Maybe you go to your workplace when you're contagious, simply crossing your fingers that you don't get anyone else sick while using over-the-counter medications to reduce your symptoms. Or when you feel emotionally off-kilter and in need of self-nurturing, you might find yourself giving in to others' insistence that you put your needs aside and take care of theirs first.

One reason why you experience imbalance and poor health is because you're affected by other people—and your unaddressed issues can likewise send others into a state of agitation and distress in response. If you're sick or in need of emotional nurturing or a mental break and you don't take care of yourself, everyone around you can suffer as a result.

The challenge is to reject the idea that you live in isolation and instead embrace wholeliness to improve the well-being of whomever you're in contact with. You can actually fend off illness and disease by balancing your thoughts and emotions and nurturing your spirit. And whenever you address your own physical, emotional, mental, or spiritual needs, all of society benefits. Your health contributes to the health of all who are interconnected in the fabric of reality.

Have you ever wondered why a disease like cancer, which is not contagious, has spread like wildfire throughout the world? Well, be it positive or negative, the energy of each person is being transmitted to others constantly. (This concept is similar to the butterfly effect that I discussed earlier.) That's why someone who serves as a caretaker to another who is sick might eventually end up ill, too. Also, the more one person unleashes hatred, anger, jealousy, or bitterness upon others, the greater the chance that these negative emotions will manifest as physical illness for himself and anyone in his sphere.

Similarly, it turns out that war, loss, and abuse affect not just the people directly involved, but those who know and are in contact with them. Suffering can be a legacy if we don't work to resolve our karma. All of us need to make sure our interactions with others are as healthy as possible, and observe how being exposed to strife can alter our own mental, emotional, and physical states.

• • •

If you are on the path to wellness and are eating more healthfully, your mind will respond with fewer mood swings and improved mental clarity (no more "brain fog"). When you attempt to mend your soul through connecting to Spirit, your body will respond with improved health and more vigor. This will also cause you to be less susceptible to other people's negative energy.

That is to say, in order to attain wholeliness and work on yourself at all levels, you can begin by doing the following: take better care of your body, practice techniques for managing your emotions, consciously choose to think optimistically, and perform spiritual rituals that help you strengthen your connections to all. Each of these acts will result in healing at all levels, but you may wish to begin with the area that requires the most attention. Perhaps you're having aches and pains, your emotions seem out of control, or you've come to recognize that your interior dialogue is very pessimistic and self-critical. Whatever your main concern may be, you'll be inspired by how effective it is to address your well-being no matter where you concentrate your efforts. You'll be excited to realize that you can actually create psychosomatic health (*psyche* relates to the mind, and *somatic* means "relating to the body") rather than psychosomatic illness.

In fact, all illness is ultimately psychosomatic, but this does *not* mean that it's "all in your head" and doesn't actually exist. It's very real in the world of the senses because humans create it. Remember, your mind is connected to all other minds. Therefore, if there's a disturbance or disharmony in the collective consciousness, it may directly affect you even if you've worked to keep your own mind clear of mental and emotional toxins. If you turn on the television and learn about a distressing event that's happening on the other side of the world, you will experience distress, too, even if only subtly. This is why it's so easy to become pessimistic if you watch too many disturbing news programs or continually listen to depressing music.

Any type of condition involves a disconnection of some sort, a separation or rift that needs mending so wholeliness can be achieved. You may be disconnected from thoughts that need to be brought into your conscious mind—or disconnected from your body, ignoring signals alerting you that you aren't attending to its needs.

Being healthy in mind, body, and spirit is sacred because when you feel complete, you're closer to the Divine and all creation. While it may seem paradoxical, the key to well-being and harmony is striving to be happy and accepting your life as it is right now.

As you work toward wholeliness, your body will start to repair itself and your heart will mend as you experience compassion and forgiveness. Your mind will let go of its anxiety and become expansive in its thinking as it opens to new possibilities—your creativity will flow. All those problems that used to weigh you down will no longer overwhelm you because you'll be filled with enthusiasm and energy. Positivity will reach you on all levels.

Our Disconnected Approach to Health

When we're not feeling well, we tend to look for solutions that don't cost too much time and money. This attitude is encouraged by companies or medical professionals who are getting rich by promoting these quick fixes. Taking a pill or undergoing surgery often does yield fast, seemingly positive results. Addressing an ailment through nutritional intervention, exercise, and other stress-relieving techniques, combined with practices that help us face and resolve karmic issues affecting our thoughts and emotions—all of these take time, effort, and commitment.

Because we fear sickness and death, those only interested in profits can easily frighten us into using expedient but unhealthy approaches to well-being. Such approaches don't take wholeliness into account, and they don't serve us in the long run because they don't examine the imbalances of the entire system. By looking at the physical ailment but not the emotional stress that's manifesting the ailment, we're ensuring that the problem will return.

You're meant to look at the big picture of well-being, the *whole* of it. Your very wise, intuitive mind will alert you to the fact that something is wrong. Don't be embarrassed to report to your doctor that you sense something is "off" but don't know how to describe it. It's important not to disregard your nonphysical symptoms, even though they can't be remedied with a pill or surgery. In Ayurvedic medicine, the imbalances that result in fatigue, malaise, and mood swings are considered ailments appropriate for a physician to address, just as he'd address a rash or a broken bone. If your doctor thinks that such approaches have no validity, you might want to begin working with healers who employ more holistic methods.

Your body may alert you to an imbalance long before you actually become ill, but like many people, you've probably learned to ignore its inconvenient signals to slow down and attend to your needs. For example, you should be experiencing hunger when you need to eat and fullness when you've had enough, but do you in fact eat when you're feeling angry or emotionally distressed or starve yourself in order to keep your weight down? Or perhaps you dismiss the mild stomach cramps or other feelings of physical discomfort that arise whenever you consume particular foods, not realizing that this is a clear indication from your body that these items aren't right for your system. It can be much easier to fall into the habit of taking medications for heartburn or indigestion instead of revamping your diet. There are plenty of advertisements for antacids, but how many do you see that remind you to eat fiber and cruciferous vegetables? Unfortunately, our culture encourages a disconnection from the body's needs. Have you internalized this unhealthy message?

If you push past your body's warnings, the consequences may be mild at first, but over time they can become more severe. A client of mine had digestive issues for years before she finally was in such physical agony that she ended up in an emergency room and was diagnosed with celiac disease (an allergy to wheat and certain other grains that is becoming more common these days, even though many people choose to ignore the discomfort that's alerting them to check out the cause of the imbalance in their bodies).

If you simply medicate away high blood pressure, treat the symptoms of hypoglycemia by eating more sugar, and ignore the excess weight you've gained, you may eventually develop type 2 diabetes. This disease is genetic but triggered by lifestyle choices (unlike type 1 diabetes, which is not related to lifestyle and mostly affects children and young people, but also adults)—and if left untreated, it can result in blindness, heart disease, stroke, neuropathy (nerve death), and more.

The number of preventable cases of diabetes has exploded in the West, yet too many of us continue to turn deaf ears to our bodies' cries for balance. Type 2 diabetes, like any disease, has a psychological component (genetics) and a karmic cause. But we must *never* blame individuals for developing any disease or try to make them feel guilty for the choices they've made. To be judgmental and blame someone for an illness is to cause further disconnection from each other and create bad karma that affects us all.

Karmic Lessons in Disease

Both individually and as part of a larger community, we need to look at our afflictions and ask what karmic lessons we might learn from them. With diabetes, for instance, perhaps the question is, "Why look to food to provide the sweetness of life that can only be found in wholeliness?" On a karmic level, diabetes may be appearing in the human species so that we're forced to face how we've disconnected from the whole and looked to satisfy our desire for "sweetness" in the wrong way. Also, managing this condition requires discipline and self-awareness, but our culture promotes indulgence and a lack of introspection. As more people find life sweeter by living harmoniously with others and savoring their nourishing connection to the Divine, we may be able to finally see a decline in the number of cases of diabetes.

We also need to take a closer look at the karmic reasons behind all conditions to examine what's creating them. At their root, many diseases have to do with inflammation, which is often associated with anger . . . why are we all so angry? Why do we think that it's okay to constantly be upset even though we know that this has a toxic effect on the body? What messages about this emotion are we receiving from our neighbors, friends, religion, community, and culture? Are they healthy messages?

Autoimmune disorders are diseases of disconnection—that is, one part of your body becomes disconnected from another. Why is it that certain parts of the body don't recognize when other parts need help? There's definitely a lesson about wholeliness here. If you have an autoimmune disorder, this could be because your mind is disconnected from your body, emotions, or spirit. Addressing this unhealthy rift will help you move toward wellness.

Although of course we all want the best health for ourselves and our loved ones, we share a common responsibility to begin healing the imbalances in our culture so that we can eradicate disease. Behind every disease there exists a karmic explanation. As more of us strive for wholeliness, we'll start to resolve our individual and group karma and, eventually, we'll see these diseases disappear.

It's also important to note here that although karma from your past lives is imprinted on your genes, your genes aren't the only factor influencing your physical health. The new scientific field of epigenetics is looking at gene expression and seeking to answer the question, "Why do some genes remain dormant while others become active?"

Genes that are responsible for developing illness are far more likely to become active if there's an imbalance present in your body or mind. It's similar to being more vulnerable to catching a cold if you're under a lot of pressure. By taking care of your physical well-being, reducing emotional stress, and focusing on thoughts that generate a sense of happiness and harmony, you may be able to prevent these genes from expressing. *Understand that all illnesses are stress related.* A harmful genetic predisposition shouldn't be seen as a "curse," but as a karmic obstacle that you can overcome. When you eliminate stress and work on your karma, you become less likely to develop disease, even if you have a genetic predisposition.

On the other hand, creating new negative karma can impact your body at a cellular level and influence your genes to the point that something unwanted develops. This disease or condition can then make its way to the next generation—your children—by remaining in your DNA. Everything within your multifaceted self possesses a memory, and this includes your genes.

If one of your parents suffers from a genetic disorder and you inherit it, don't believe that you deserve to suffer from the same debilitating issue in the future. You inherited this gene because you're meant to resolve your family's karma.

You may also become sick because someone around you has created bad karma that you've taken on, put toxins into the environment you share, or caused you severe emotional stress. If this person emits toxic energy or is ill, you may have chosen to absorb these things in order to resolve individual and group karma—but know that this is a large burden to take on, and few people do it. Only very evolved souls tend to make this choice for the good of the whole. For example, Christianity teaches that God became man in the form of Jesus in order to suffer with humans and resolve the karma of our species through sacrifice.

Some souls actually incarnate in the visible world, as humans or animals, for the purpose of sacrificing for others. I will never forget the day after Virgil was diagnosed with lung cancer, and one of our cats lay down on his bed next to him and did not move for an entire 12 hours (and this cat did not even particularly like my husband). I sensed that our pet was absorbing his sick energy by being next to him. The next day, we found the cat mysteriously dead on the corner of our street. Also, right after the cancer was diagnosed and Virgil was given just months to live, we noticed that our dog started to grow a lump on her head. Unbelievably, as the lump continued to grow, Virgil's tumor started to shrink! Inexplicably, our dog died around the time my husband was supposed to have lost his battle with cancer. I believe that our pets soaked up the cancerous energy in order to sacrifice themselves for their owner. Animals can be incredibly selfless creatures.

You may not intend to take on others' dark energy and suffer for them, so it's important to shield yourself from such negativity. Set up a protective wall by imagining yourself surrounded by Divine white light. It's like creating a sort of bubble for yourself through which no harmful energy can penetrate. While you don't have control over the individual and group karma you were born with, you can make it easier to resolve by avoiding emotional and mental toxins that could overwhelm your ability to process it all.

• • •

When a spirit reincarnates, it does so in a state of amnesia about how difficult it is to handle the emotional toxins and stresses of life on Earth—which, as I'm sure you're aware, can be quite a struggle. But I've often seen cases where someone has spiritually given up on this world because dealing with her karma turns out to be too overwhelming. She "checks out" emotionally and mentally via depression, mental confusion, or even dementia or Alzheimer's; then her body gives out by creating disease and illness that eventually claims her. When the spirit doesn't want to be here, the mind and body heed its call to withdraw from this life.

Sometimes there's an internal struggle between the desires of the spirit and mind and the pull of the body's primitive survival instinct. If you're meant to die young, you may know this at a soul level, but you may also attempt to use logic to deny this reality, and your body may resist giving in to this outcome that you were meant to experience.

Many years ago, I spent hours drafting complex astrological charts for my mother, which revealed her karma and destiny. As I pored over them, I realized that they all indicated that she would die when she was 64. I didn't want to believe this, but even though I knew my calculations were accurate, I checked and checked again, only to find that they agreed. When my mother reached that age, we were involved in a terrible car accident— but despite the seriousness of her injuries, she recovered. Yet she spent the next seven years as an invalid, slowly deteriorating. I believe she was meant to die in that crash, but her body, mind, and spirit resisted her destiny. Perhaps she wished to remain here with her family just a bit longer.

The mind's influence on the body is extremely powerful. In fact, it's so powerful that if you believe that a certain pill can cure you of a disease or ailment, taking it may produce positive effects even if that pill is simply a placebo (an inert medication, such as a sugar pill, that the patient thinks is actual medication). The power isn't in the pill, but in your belief in it. If you understand the concept of the placebo effect, you can learn to heal yourself without the help of any remedy.

However, because the causes of sickness can be complex and involve the karma of many people, your mind may not be enough to allow you to heal yourself at a physical level. When that happens, it's because physical healing wasn't meant to take place for reasons you may never know. Regardless, you should always attempt to use your mental ability to try to heal yourself at all levels of your being.

Caring for Others . . . and Yourself

Physical illness often begins with emotional anxiety, which can damage the body at the cellular level. Many caretakers become sick or develop diseases as a result of the emotional challenge of constantly being around people who are seriously ill. They're creating good karma by lovingly caring for the old and sick, even when the person they're caring for isn't the most pleasant. Yet the stress of taking on the responsibility of another person's life, of having to be at someone's side during a difficult time, can be very intense.

Emotional and mental toxins are unavoidable in these types of situations. If you're in this role, you'll naturally have moments of anger, sorrow, resentment, or fear, because tending to someone who has major health issues (and is perhaps also depressed) can vacuum the energy out of you. Fortunately, there are ways to make this serious responsibility, or any other, seem less demanding: You can accept that stress is part of the experience and consciously choose not to dwell on the frustrations; or you can constantly remind yourself of the good you're doing, and shower yourself with love and compassion.

If you lose your temper or become disheartened, forgive yourself immediately and reconnect to the Divine through prayer. Do ask for help from friends and family, but forgive anyone who can't give you what you need due to his or her own weaknesses. And take care of your physical body, even if that means not doing as much for the one you're caring for as you feel you should. In this way, you can make it through this temporary situation without creating bad karma or being overcome by negativity that just creates more stress.

I cared for both my mother and my husband when they were sick, and believe me, I understand the frustration. I've been through the spoon-feeding, the bed changing, and the sponge baths. I would even gently dab the sweat off of their foreheads as they slept. Instead of allowing resentment to build up inside over the struggle you find yourself in, try what I did: thank the Divine that your loved one is still with you and that you've been given this opportunity to express love; develop greater strength, patience, and tolerance; and potentially heal your own karma. If you didn't have a good relationship with the individual you're caring for, recognize how powerful this act of selfless caretaking is. Appreciate what a giving, generous person you are.

Every day, before beginning the daily routine of caring for someone who is sick or dependent on you, such as a disabled spouse or a special-needs child, pray for him or her and for yourself. Pray to the Divine that today be less challenging, and that there will be improvements, even if they're small. Most of all, ask for the strength to feel the presence of Spirit supporting the souls of both you and your "patient." Caretaking, although a demanding task, can truly bring you closer to the person you love.

• • •

Whether you're caring for another or just looking after yourself, don't underestimate how important it is to feed your emotional needs by clearing your mind of negative thoughts and replacing them with optimistic and cheerful ones. Know what activities make you feel lighter and more energized, and engage in them. Don't intend to get around to taking care of yourself—do it! Sing if it makes you feel happy. Read positive stories about good people healing the bad karma in the world. Detach from sad realities through pleasant distractions and small acts of kindness toward yourself.

To keep your emotional state balanced and healthy, try to stay aware of your hidden beliefs, emotions, and thoughts, and take the time to get in touch with why you're feeling uncomfortable. In this way, you can correct your thinking and let go of your difficult emotions, replacing them with joy and hope.

So many people today are angry and churning with negative thoughts. It's very important to take time out to be in silence, away from the images, words, or individuals who stimulate anger. Even if you're an extrovert who thrives on stimulation, you still need downtime to avoid being caught up in destructive habits of the mind. If you're always on the go or at the center of drama, it may be because you're afraid of slowing down and facing your painful emotions.

We each require the space to interact with ourselves and no one else. It becomes all too easy to forget the true nature of our *self* when we're constantly feeling that we must force a smile for our boss, be extra cheerful around our kids, act lovingly around our spouse, or make small talk with friends. Too often the self becomes second to the "act" that each of us must put on for the outside world.

Emotional support is very important for maintaining balance. Friends and family can be hugely supportive, but pets can also provide wonderful emotional support because they offer unconditional love. If you don't have a pet, try to spend some time around animals by offering to care for a co-worker's dog while she's away. And if you do have animals, don't use them as an excuse to avoid your issues or stay at home. I know it can be easy to appreciate animals more than humans because they're so innocent. But *people* help you face your karma, as you're meant to.

And in your relationships, always give and take. Imbalances lead to anger and hurt feelings, which cause disturbances in the heart. Find supportive individuals, and nourish your relationships with them.

When your sadness, frustration, or anger builds up, cry. Despite its bad reputation, crying is a tremendously powerful release of energy, and one that is necessary from time to time. After you've shed tears, your mind will be free to focus on something positive.

A Balanced, Natural Approach to Wellness

Surgery and medications—the twin approaches to health favored by Western medicine—both violate the physical self and ignore the sacred connections between the body, mind, and spirit that can be used to create health and healing. In surgery, flesh and organs are cut and separated; tumors are removed along with surrounding tissue; and joints are replaced with foreign, artificial substances. Medications, whether prescribed or over-the-counter, are derived from unnatural substances, and then their molecules are altered in a laboratory so the manufacturer can claim a patent.

The body doesn't recognize these artificial substances and is confused by what is clearly not of nature.

All parts of the body are connected in complex ways that are still not fully understood. If you turn away from natural means of healing, you'll usually find that it's as difficult to balance your system as it is for the smartest scientist to return an ecosystem to balance after it's been ravaged. You'll probably experience side effects from drugs because these substances are not natural and therefore don't agree with you the way a piece of food or an herb would. You may even respond to them in unexpected ways—in fact, side effects can sometimes be worse than the original ailment. Furthermore, not all reactions to drugs are known, especially when it comes to those that are new to the market.

Another consequence of using pharmaceuticals to treat physical or emotional imbalances is that they cause the body to forget its own healing wisdom. When you put powerful medications into your body as substitutes for natural substances or to artificially enhance processes, you can cause imbalances. For example, if you use human-made hormones in place of the ones you're no longer producing, then after the course of medication ends, your body is likely to forget what it could create in the first place.

If your chemistry is out of whack, it needs to be rebalanced, not shocked by more drugs. With holistic treatments—addressing your stress, karma, and entire physical system in a natural way— you can gently coax your body into functioning as it's supposed to. Then it can use its own wisdom to once again generate the hormones you need in the proper amounts.

Similar to this, you can build up a resistance to antibiotics if you overuse them. The bacteria that have evolved to withstand attacks from common antibiotics can infect other people. Even though when you're sick you're likely to be more concerned about your own health than other people's, your use of drugs does affect everyone on this planet.

When you're under extreme physical or emotional stress, medication can be a temporary part of your healing treatments, but it should never be the first resort . . . after all, it's very likely to do more harm than good. Energy healing, being in nature, exposing yourself to sunlight, eating a more balanced diet, getting enough sleep—more and more, researchers are coming to recognize that these simple methods are quite often much more effective than drugs. In times of tremendous anxiety or sadness, turn first to techniques for the mind, body, and spirit. For example, the herb Saint-John's-wort and regular physical exercise are both highly effective in treating depression.

When you're ill, it may take time and care to bring yourself back to a state of wellness, but your immune system is meant to keep you healthy despite the daily assault of toxins, bacteria, and viruses. Recognize that you're facing an opportunity not just for recovery at all levels, but also to contribute to the well-being of the whole by bringing balance into your small corner of the fabric of reality.

Doing Your Part to Bring Wholeliness into the World

As a society, we need to be more accommodating of human afflictions, whether they be diseases, mental illnesses, or spiritual dilemmas that cause emotional crises. We should have schools that can work with hyperactive children rather than insisting that they be medicated to make them "fit in." We need rituals for processing grief, which is a natural part of life, rather than drugs that stop the flow of emotion. We'd also benefit from workplaces that are less stressful, so employees wouldn't feel chronically anxious because their co-workers and bosses are engaging in conflict instead of cooperation.

Our impatience and intolerance toward each other (and ourselves) is producing real problems, which we vainly try to manage through artificial means. All of us are suffering from the stigma of not meeting others' expectations, which are often unrealistic and unfair in the first place. The internal pressure to be perfect and never let anyone down causes tremendous emotional stress; eventually, the body responds by manifesting illness.

Like everyone, you're profoundly affected by these values but probably don't realize it. When the little voice inside your head says that you should feel guilty or ashamed for being imbalanced, and should "get over it" as quickly as possible, recognize that you've internalized values that are not in sync with wholeliness. Healing takes time, patience, and insight into our connections between body, mind, spirit, and environment.

Collectively, human beings need to embrace wholeliness by fostering health and well-being for all. We could do this if we'd just be willing to provide better access to alternative healing methods that take into account the totality of a person and his or her experiences. Instead, by overvaluing material wealth, we've created health-care systems that serve those seeking to make a profit rather than those who are sick and in need.

As populations age, we have to start thinking about how we'll look after the elderly with dignity and grace. Because wholeliness involves balance, attending to the needs of the sick or dying is not solely an act of giving but one of receiving as well. It offers the gifts of patience, humility, and insight into our ability to affect others for the better—and these are gifts *we* receive when we value the health of others and work to bring them back to a state of well-being.

If you're feeling lonely and disconnected, you'd do well to spend time with those in hospitals and nursing homes, as this would help you realize that you're capable of lifting the spirits of someone who is frail or ill. You'll find that caring for others who can't care for themselves is sacred work that will help you with the inner thoughts and emotions that weigh you down. It nurtures the soul because it brings you back to an awareness of wholeliness and the harmony between giving and receiving love. It reminds you of your power to affect others, along with their ability to uplift you, and gives you a sense of purpose.

How do you work at healing *yourself?* Through techniques such as praying, meditating, listening to your intuition, and carefully contemplating your choices; as well as through eating quality foods that have been grown and sold in a way that is respectful to the earth and all its creatures. Energy-healing techniques, natural supplements, regular exercise, spending time in nature—the list of wholesome, life-affirming, healing techniques is a long one.

As you embrace the ideal of bringing wholeliness into the world, remember that you can make a difference by limiting the chemicals and drugs you use, because they eventually end up in the environment. Even if you flush expired pills down the toilet, or dump them into landfills, they don't just disappear; they enter the ecosystem. And keep in mind that everything you eat that isn't organic is in some way contaminated, whether it's by pesticides, artificial hormones, or antibiotics. Thus, when you eat organic foods you contribute to the health of the earth and all those who dwell here.

You also contribute to the health of all when you avoid using chemicals in your home, such as for cleaning. The compounds created in a laboratory to ensure that your eggs don't stick to your frying pan, for instance, or the ingredients used in insect repellent are extremely harmful. Such complex manufactured molecules don't magically disappear from the planet when they're washed down a drain or returned to the soil as part of your waste—they simply move from object to human body to water, earth, sky, and so on. Of course, the human body is marvelously designed to rid itself of toxins, and there are many ways you can enhance this cleansing process, but the number of poisons and synthetic materials you and others are exposed to is great. Vow to do your part to live more simply, for your own sake as well as that of Mother Earth and all her inhabitants.

The Future of Health

Every day more people are embracing wholeliness and the path of wellness. In the coming years, we're going to see astonishing breakthroughs that will incorporate holistic healing methods that work with the body, are in sync with wholeliness, build upon our sacred connections, and don't involve separation or imbalance.

Energy medicine is going to become more mainstream. (Acupuncture is already covered by many private health-insurance plans, which is a tiny but important step in the right direction.)

You'll see more use of its techniques for balancing at the levels of mind, body, and spirit. As humans increasingly become inspired by wholeliness to recognize the importance of having a healthy energy field, energy healers will be more common. Today a healer can tap into your energy, "see" where the problem is located in your field, and then address it. She may manipulate energy with her hands or by utilizing sound, such as the resonance of singing bowls. She's even able to use her skills nonlocally to bring about great results, working on her patients who may be in a different town or state.

Because of their holistic approach, energy healers often ask their clients about what's going on emotionally and physically and where they are in their lives. They know what ailments are common in women who are in adolescence or menopause, and what types of diseases and illnesses affect those individuals who have repressed their anger or pain. For example, one healer told me that my husband had lung cancer because of lingering guilt that he hadn't been able to save his mother, who had died many years before in a horrible car accident. Realistically, Virgil knew that there was nothing he could have done—he hadn't been there or even known that his mother was going for a drive—yet irrational guilt was lodged in his subconscious. Soon after his mother died, he began smoking, which is a behavior that brought on a physical weakness in the same way the persistent thought *Maybe I could have done something for her* created an imbalance at the level of the mind.

When an energy healer reads your energy field, he commonly finds imbalances. He senses or sees the places where the structures of energy—the spinning chakras along the spine—are not healthy, clear, or moving freely. He knows that what starts as an emotional disturbance eventually becomes a physical one. This is why a medical intuitive can examine you months before you develop an issue in the body and predict that, without intervention, you will experience a heart attack, stroke, blood disorder, or other serious disease.

Each of the chakras that an energy healer works with is associated with certain organs or systems of the body, such as the digestive and circulatory systems. Again, your physical self is uni-fied with the spiritual self, which is contained within the energy that surrounds you. The chakras are also associated with particu-lar mind-sets and emotional states. And just as the body and its fluids need to flow freely, emotions must come and go, chakras have to move without impediment, and *chi*—that is, your vital energy contained within your energy field—needs to circulate.

● ● ●

The energy medicine that will be available in the future will include more sophisticated forms of laser surgery, which is al-ready being used to cure problems with eyesight, teeth, and skin. New techniques will be used in ways we haven't yet imagined. Instead of going under the knife or bombarding the body with manufactured chemicals, you'll be able to take advantage of less-invasive methods that utilize light. Lasers will even be used to treat cancer, targeting the growth of malignant cells and shrink-ing them in size.

Also, more vaccines will be available that work with the body's natural memory. Those used to prevent certain viruses and diseas-es that increase the risk of cancer are already being administered, such as the ones used for human papillomavirus (HPV), which causes cervical cancer, and hepatitis B, which causes liver cancer.

As a whole, you'll see more acceptance of the fact that health and a spiritual connection to the Divine are inseparable and essen-tial, and you'll have many more holistic healing methods avail-able to you.

In addition, there will be more support for eating better as people begin to change the way they view their diet choices. Right now, many individuals shop and eat without regard to wholeliness; that is, they don't tend to concern themselves with how we're *all* affected by the way food is raised and made available to us. We're about to go beyond learning a bit about nutrition or eating right and understand that the foods we choose and the grocery stores we patronize play a vital role in everyone's health and the health of our planet.

You'll also benefit from a major shift from an illness model of health to a wellness model that incorporates holistic treatments and prevention. As the human race comes to value this approach at all levels—and appreciates that everyone's physical, mental, and spiritual well-being influences others—you'll find it much easier to remain in balance *yourself.*

In the meantime, you can begin working on your body today through healing your mind and nurturing your spirit. You can calm your negative emotions through relaxation, exercise, and eating foods that support a positive mood. As I said, healing at any level—body, mind, or spirit—brings about improvements at all the other levels due to the holistic nature of your being. So balance the amount of attention and care you devote to each, and you'll begin to experience more peace, power, and vitality.

How to Achieve Wholeliness of Body, Mind, and Spirit

Observe

Look at the connections between your mind, body, and spirit. How do you feel emotionally when you eat unhealthy, processed food? In turn, how do you feel when you eat healthy, unprocessed food? And how does it feel to buy food from a farmer or a food co-op that gives extra food to the local shelter?

Where in your body or energy field do you have difficulties when you're insecure, angry, or sad?

When are you at your healthiest and most vital? Is it when you've recharged your system with wholesome nutrients?

Which activities energize you and make you feel physically strong and connected to your body in a positive way? Which ones make you feel joyous and exuberant?

Be sure to record your observations in your journal to help you remember what you need to do in order to feel good at every level.

Pray

Pray for health, well-being, and balance for yourself—as well as for all the world's people and creatures, and for Mother Earth herself. Ask for access to the wisdom of your body so that it may defend against diseases without your having to resort to artificial drugs. Pray to recognize how you, other people, and the environment affect each other so that you can correct imbalances and bring about wholeliness. Embrace your connection to the Divine in your body, mind, and spirit.

Also, pray that others begin to see the sacred relationship between body, mind, and spirit so that they take better care of themselves. Ask that they might relinquish their anger, frustration, and hatred and understand what an impact their negative emotions are having upon the world.

Pray for healers so that they too may enjoy health and well-being and continue their important and sacred healing work.

Act

Action takes place outside of you. While it's important to have a rich inner life of thoughts and emotions, it's easy to become stuck in your head and forget the importance of following through on your positive intentions. If you have to write on your calendar or set reminders in your phone to act in ways that support your physical, mental, and spiritual well-being, do it. Don't let another day go by without making your dream of a healthier life begin to unfold.

To help get you started, I've made the following list to recap what I covered in this chapter and get you thinking about your first step toward wellness:

— **Eat healthy, organic foods.** When you buy and eat locally grown foods, you're reducing pollution and using less of the earth's energy resources. You make it easier for the soil to cleanse itself of toxins and provide healthy crops. Purchase food from farmers' markets, health-food stores, and food co-ops. Try your hand at gardening. Even a few fresh, homegrown herbs and vegetables combined with whole grains will improve your diet.

— **Avoid processed foods and excess sugar, salt, and fat.** Your body looks at processed junk foods as alien substances. If it could speak, it would ask you, "What the heck is this?" But since it can't, it does the next best thing: it transforms such "food" into fat and stores it for future use. Note that these items have also lost almost all of their nutritional value—and without adequate vitamins and minerals, your body can't carry out its most essential functions.

By doing your own cooking, it's easier to avoid toxins. If you're short on time, prepare a larger meal so that you can eat the leftovers for a few days at a time. (Remember to consume your vegetables raw or only slightly steamed or grilled whenever possible. Boiling them causes most of the vitamins and minerals to seep out.)

— **Be conscious of the true cost of your food.** Factory farms that mistreat animals and cut corners on safety are more likely to produce contaminated foods. It's worth paying extra to support a system that benefits you, the farmers, and the earth.

— **Drink plenty of water.** Your body is mostly made of water, so it's vital to be constantly replenishing your fluids—eight glasses a day is a must. I also recommend investing in an alkaline water filter. The pH level in your body is very delicate, and too much acidity can create imbalances and illness.

Skip those afternoon sodas: the sugar in them can dehydrate you, and the artificial sweeteners in diet products are not digestible at all. And be aware that most juices aren't even made from fruits. Only buy the ones that are clearly marked 100% JUICE and NOT FROM CONCENTRATE. Make your own bubbly drink by mixing pure orange juice with sparkling water.

— **Work out regularly.** Exercise for overall health and to sweat out toxins. Yoga and tai chi are especially helpful forms of movement because they promote mental discipline and the flow of energy within the body. In addition, make movement part of your life in small ways. Taking a flight of stairs rather than the elevator boosts circulation, works the heart muscle, keeps the bodily fluids moving, and leads to healthier bones. You can also park your car farther away from your office, or get off the train one stop before the store and walk an extra 15 minutes.

— **Break bread with others.** Nourish your emotional and intellectual life, as well as your soul, by sharing meals with others. Eat with people you care about and those you'd like to get to know better. Prepare meals together with friends or family members, including your children, so that dinnertime is a special part of the day when everyone is in one room enjoying each other's company. This will create memories that will remain with you forever.

— **Send love to your body.** Focus on the part of you that is hurting or imbalanced. Place your hands over the spot, and send loving energy into your body. You may feel a warm, tingling sensation as you do so, because you're effectively transmitting positive energy to a wounded area. This type of healing is the basis of Reiki, just one of the many forms of energy healing.

— **Speak lovingly about yourself.** Whether you express your thoughts aloud or not, notice whether you think about yourself in a positive or negative way. Replace harsh self-judgments with reminders of your strengths and attributes. Instead of thinking *I hate growing old and feeling aches and pains,* be grateful for your health and say, "I'm so glad I'm taking excellent care of my wonderful, healthy body."

— **Reduce emotional and mental toxins.** In addition to eliminating the habit of harshly judging yourself, which causes emotional and mental toxins, reduce your exposure to negative people. If someone's depressed, be compassionate and urge her to get help—but don't get pulled down into a lower vibration. Recharge yourself by spending time around positive people and engaging in activities that make you feel joyful. Otherwise, your emotions will become imbalanced.

You may also find therapy useful, but be certain that your therapist helps you go beyond simply identifying your problems and actually begins to heal your patterns.

— **Meditate.** There are many forms of meditation that are effective for bringing about well-being at all levels of the body. Practice regularly, particularly whenever you're feeling imbalanced or upset, even if you spend just a few minutes focusing on your breathing and freeing your mind of negative thoughts. Meditation is like calming a tumultuous river so that the waters flow peacefully again.

— **Get outside!** You need sunshine in order to generate vitamin D, which is vital for physical health, and manufacture serotonin. So try to spend time in nature every day, or at least exercise outdoors. If you're forced to spend the day inside, bring nature to you with windows and natural lighting, plants, and pets that remind you of your connection to the earth.

— **Work with energy healers.** There are many healers who can help you change your energy field, which will benefit you emotionally, mentally, and physically.

— **Listen to your body and your intuition.** Take the time to pay attention to signals that you need to change what you're ingesting, whether it's food that doesn't agree with you or negative news that upsets your equilibrium and erodes your optimism. Everything you see, touch, smell, taste, hear, and sense carries a certain vibration that influences you, so make sure that you only let positive influences hold your attention.

— **Turn to the Divine.** Spirit is an endless source of love to help you heal and foster your well-being. Research shows that prayer has mental and physical health benefits, but this isn't the only way to communicate with Source. Try using other techniques that help you feel Spirit's presence and draw on Divine power to support you in maintaining good health.

As you begin to understand your sacred connections to all levels of who you are (the physical, the mental, and the spiritual), and between yourself and the visible and invisible worlds, your perception will begin to shift. Your ego will stop dominating your thinking, and you'll come to see that the challenges you face are not designed to punish you but to awaken you to resolve your karma and heal internally. You'll experience wellness as you acknowledge and cultivate the relationship of your mind, body, spirit, and environment. If you release your ego's illusions, which make you feel disconnected and resentful of the suffering that you've gone through, you can then open your mind to more challenging approaches.

In the next part of the book, you'll discover how your limited understanding of time, religion, and science has held you back—and, by extension, caused you to participate in resisting human evolution.

Although it may be difficult to let go of ideas that you've believed in for a lifetime, this shift is vital because it will allow you to experience wholeness internally. You will no longer feel victimized by the passage of time, and your spirituality will be set free from the limitations imposed upon it by the teachings of religion and science. By shifting your perspective, your world will begin to change.

•• ● ••

PART III

NEW
VIEWS

CHAPTER

8

A NEW VIEW
OF TIME

"Because the rhythms and patterns of nature
tell us precisely when we can expect the repeating cycles
of the past, they also tell us when we have the greatest opportunity
to change the hurtful and destructive patterns of the past—
the choice points—that create the new cycles of life!"

— GREGG BRADEN

Human beings developed our ideas about time in order to make sense of our experiences in the visible world, where our senses tell us what is real. Although time itself can't be seen or heard, we experience it through our senses: we feel its effects on our bodies and witness proof of it when we see the sun setting or rising and the seasons changing.

Yet according to Plato, separate from the world of the senses is a place where infinite, pure forms exist. He was speaking of the invisible world, where there is perfect beauty, justice, and truth. Wholeliness teaches us that we shouldn't ignore the invisible world because it is part of the whole of reality. And in this realm, there is no need to calculate years, months, days, hours, or seconds. Time operates quite differently.

Plato believed that true intelligence is the ability to understand on this level, to recognize that what we've created in the visible world is always an inferior copy of those perfect forms. For example, the chair I sit on has only one form—but in the invisible world, beyond the tangible, there exists every chair that ever existed and every concept and theory of what a chair could be all at the same time. There is no "chair that once was" or "chair that will be some-day." Such distinctions make no sense in the invisible world.

We can apply Plato's concept to see how time works. The invis-ible world contains all possibilities—past, present, and future—at once. Here in the realm beyond the tangible, everything that has happened, is happening, and will happen are all commingled into one reality. Our ideas about time are the result of our limited ways of comprehending the perfection in the invisible realm. Time is a construct that doesn't accurately reflect the relationship between events. As Henry Van Dyke wrote:

Time is
Too slow for those who wait,
Too swift for those who fear,
Too long for those who grieve,
Too short for those who rejoice;
But for those who love,
Time is
Eternity.

Seeing Beyond the Now

The rational mind struggles to grasp the idea that our percep-tion creates time, and that there's a world where past, present, and future exist all at once and blend into each other. In con-trast, we can actually experience these truths. Those of us with psychic abilities are able to go beyond our notion of linear time, in which the past is always behind us and the future is always ahead of us.

Now, although I do have especially powerful intuitive gifts, I believe that all people can—and do!—enter this realm of infinite forms that breaks linear time (transcends the limits of time). Intuition allows us to see connections that may not seem to make sense in the visible world, but scientists have told us that phenomena such as precognitive dreams and déjà vu are meaningless coincidences or tricks of the mind. Yet as someone who is able to break linear time, I know that these explanations are false. I can actually see events in the distant past or future, usually ones that involve me—or an incarnation of me—but I can see other people, such as strangers for whom I'm doing a session.

For example, I was recently reminded of some predictions I'd made 20 years ago for a woman named Maggie. I told her that she'd marry her soul mate, a wealthy man she already knew; her financial troubles would end; and she'd even have enough money to start a charity. But I stated that none of this would happen until after she moved to another state and several years had passed.

Although Maggie thought my predictions were interesting, they seemed too far-fetched and she didn't think much about them. Five years later, after graduating from college and moving across the country back to her home state, she renewed a friendship with a man who was quite wealthy, just as I'd envisioned. To her delight, she even started a charity for sick children. Why did so much time have to pass before all this came true? There's no way to know, but I can guess that Maggie was simply meant to have certain experiences before she got together with this man.

People who are willing to believe that maybe, just maybe, intuitives like me do have a special ability don't always know what to make of such a gift. Since I've been able to break linear time for most of my life, I know that there is a significance to it. Like seers of old, prophets, and medicine men and women, I'm fortunate to be capable of recognizing sacred connections between the past, present, and future—and between individuals and groups—that others can't see. I know that we are all linked in mysterious yet very real ways in this invisible realm, so when a situation looks hopeless, healing and love can pour into us from one of these relationships. We don't live in a world of random events that have no meaning, but one in which everything is part of the whole.

Seeing these connections, or at least acknowledging that they exist, helps provide a far better understanding of karma, healing, and how to end suffering by working with the shifting currents of time. It's what allows us to understand that wholeliness is our true nature.

In the visible world, we have to work within the limits of time and recognize cause and effect: something happens, which causes something else to happen as a result. According to this human-made law, what's occurring now was only influenced by events in the past, not by anything that is yet to occur. We're locked into suffering the consequences of what happened previously.

Our perception of time and the law of cause and effect help us in the visible world in certain ways. For example, if I say that I'll come by your house tonight at seven, you know exactly when that will be. Then when I push your doorbell, you'll hear a sound that tells you I've arrived. These actions occur as a result of linear time.

But in the invisible realm, these rules don't hold. Relation-ships between events are very different—what's happening now might be influenced by something in the future, and the probable future will reveal itself today. In the visible world, if the doorbell I ring doesn't work, we think it's a mechanical failure and hire someone to fix it. In the invisible world, that event has a signifi-cance we can only rarely see when our minds are focused on the visible world. For example, it may be that one of us is meant to in-teract with the doorbell repairman because there will be a benefit to that meeting.

I'm sure you can think of a similar experience in which chance seemed to bring you together with a stranger and something won-derful or healing happened as a result of that meeting. In seeing beyond this physical reality, you may not know what those con-nections are supposed to lead to.

● ● ●

As an intuitive counselor, I don't always get the whole picture when I have a glimpse of the past, present, or future of an individual I'm reading for. However, I often see enough to have a sense of the meaning. I may know that my client is meant to meet a particular person who will somehow help her in her career, in her legal dilemma, or in reaching her goal, even if I only get a picture or his or her initials in my mind.

This reminds me of an appearance I made on the Spanish-language TV network Telemundo in 2004. The woman who interviewed me asked who would be the next president of Ecuador, her home country. I told her that I knew nothing about Ecuador or its politics—but then a sharp image suddenly came to me, and I described a tall man who was about 40 years old and had light eyes (unusual in that country) and a nice smile. I also intuited that he had three children and was not a known politician. Months later, my phone began ringing nonstop with queries from Ecuador, because a university professor had just emerged as a viable candidate for the presidency, and the interviewer remembered what I'd told her. Sure enough, Rafael Correa, the dark-horse candidate who completely fit my description, became president in 2007.

Although it's always fascinating when anyone can make such a claim, I don't think we access this information because God wants others to comment, "Oh, that's interesting." The Divine helps us break linear time so that we can recognize our connections to past, present, and future events—as well as to people who seem to be strangers but are actually our brothers and sisters. I believe this particular prediction was meant to encourage the citizens of Ecuador, who dearly wanted to believe that an outsider could achieve power in their country as a result of the popular vote. I think it also came about because the Divine wants to continually remind us that we are all linked to each other in the fabric of reality, where all of consciousness resides. We must never underestimate our ability to find others to support us in enacting change.

If you can believe in wholeliness, you'll start to see such connections yourself, and even experience startling coincidences and precognition. You'll more easily hear the voice of your intuition, which has access to all realms of existence. Then it will be easier for you to trust in the perfection of the invisible world and accept that despite all you've been taught about time, your understanding of it has been all wrong!

The Nature of Time and Its Rhythms

Time is a sphere: it's complete and balanced. We describe an interval of time as a *cycle,* and say that what goes around comes around again. In nature, there are solar-flare cycles and global-warming cycles. Similarly, human beings experience karmic cycles (and women experience menstrual cycles that aren't just physical but often have an emotional element, too). Societies are meant to be innovative and push forward at times, and be contemplative and slow moving at others—but nonstop progress or permanent inertia is not natural. The present and future bear a strong resemblance to the past in many ways, because the same types of events occur in the natural rhythm of life.

We're simply fooling ourselves when we see history as gone and not worth examining, or imagine that what's ahead will be completely different from anything we've ever known. We need to recognize similarities among events and notice the patterns and the rhythms of our lives.

You may have observed cycles in your own life but dismissed them as coincidental. (For the record, there are no coincidences! All synchronicities have meaning in the invisible world.) Perhaps you've gone through phases of optimism, causing you to be very hopeful about your future at times, but then you've fallen back into doubt at others.

Know that as long as you're in balance, moving forward boldly when you're optimistic and examining your situation more closely when you're pessimistic, you're in a healthy cycle. If you work on what you need to instead of ignoring it, you can achieve a harmonious attitude and approach. However, if you don't understand a cycle, you can become stuck in a rut, experiencing the same thing over and over. You can also become burned out by constantly trying to push forward when you're meant to rest and be contemplative.

Just as the moon goes through phases and the seasons change, you have distinct eras in your life. While the past doesn't literally repeat itself, old circumstances, emotions, experiences, and relationships will come up again in your future, possibly in a slightly different form . . . and fighting these cycles is exhausting!

The key to balance, peace, and power is to work with the rhythms of nature and accept the ebb and flow of life. It's important not to remain for too long in one state of being when you're supposed to move into another one. For example, are you still holding on to the behaviors that served you when you grew up in a chaotic or abusive home, to the point that you seem to attract people and situations that echo those from your past? Or are you still resentful or bitter about someone who left you or let you go from a job? Remember that grief and anger are meant to awaken you to wholeliness and karma so that you can make a conscious choice to move into a new stage of feeling, understanding, and operating in the world. They aren't meant to imprison you.

I had a client named Sabrina who came from Europe to the United States on a short visit. I told her that her future was here—that she would remain in this country because of a man she'd meet. Indeed, Sabrina met an American named Richard, with whom she fell in love. She decided to stay in the U.S., and the two of them were eventually engaged to be married. Unfortunately, before long they had an enormous, tumultuous fight that led them to call off the wedding. Both of them were at fault, yet they refused to speak to each other or reconcile; their egos dominated their thoughts and actions, and neither was willing to let go of their feelings.

Years passed, during which I counseled both Sabrina and Richard, urging them to openly discuss the situation and release the negative emotions that they harbored internally. But despite how much they missed each other, they were both stuck in the destructive cycle of "I'm right, and you're wrong." Since the two of them were constantly thinking of each other, neither one found another partner.

Finally, after countless hours of therapy, Sabrina and Richard each acknowledged that they had been acting from their destructive egos and were living in the mistakes of the past. They realized that they needed to communicate and promote inner healing for their mutual future; after all, they still truly loved each other. Once the two of them sat down, talked, and said their apologies, they were able to settle their karmic lessons. Today, having resolved and learned from their karma, they no longer look to the painful past to direct them in their journey ahead. Seven years later, they're planning their wedding once again.

The Amazing Tools of Astrology and Numerology

Getting stuck in the past, or a stage of evolution, can happen on a larger scale as well. Ancient hurts are brought into the present as younger generations inherit the bad karma that was created long ago. If we survey human history, we'll notice that the same recurring issues arise again and again because people haven't paid enough attention to the lessons they were supposed to learn.

Fortunately, we're able to observe the cycles that affect us as individuals, humanity, and the planet. Two interconnected tools that are very helpful are numerology and astrology, which can inform us about our natural rhythms, just as psychology and hypnosis can alert us to patterns of thinking and behaving that we tend to ignore.

Ancient human beings calculated time by looking up to the sky and observing the movements of celestial bodies. They believed that the positions of the planets, moon, and sun not only provided clues as to the organization of the seasons and events, but also revealed the energies from above that influence us. Astrology and numerology were first established by the ancient Babylonians in the second millennium B.C.E., but similar practices were later created in other areas of the world. All of them are valid, but I'll focus on the Western systems, which I'm more familiar with, to explain how they help us understand the rhythms of energy that affect us all.

There's a great correlation between astrology and numerology. First, they have similar circular charts that incorporate the same themes. And in both systems, planets and numbers share particular energies. For example, Mercury is associated with the number five. Both the number and planet carry the energy of communication; intellect; mental acuity; and speedy, unimpeded movement (Mercury is the planet that travels the most quickly around the sun, and is named after the Roman messenger god). In astrology, Mercury's position in the sky at your time of birth determines your communication style. If you are adventurous, express strong opinions that are backed by intelligence, and have good communication skills, the influence of Mercury and the number five will be found in your natal charts.

Both areas of study provide explanations for the cycles in your life: When planets come into particular positions in relationship to the constellation that represents your zodiac sign, they affect you in specific ways. In numerology, when you combine the number derived from your birth date with the current day or year, it yields another number, which will influence you as well. For instance, when the planet Mercury and the number five come into play on your astrological chart or when you're calculating numerology, you'll find that your communications are smoother and your mind is sharper because you're able to process information more quickly.

As you might imagine, planets and numbers affect groups of people, too. When Mercury is in retrograde (moving in a direction contrary to that of the general motion of similar bodies), particularly on a day with an energy of five, people everywhere find that communication is slowed down, complicated, or problematic. Computers are more likely to break down during these periods, important information is prone to being misplaced, and so on.

Both numerology and astrology alert you to your cycles and give you clues about significant life events and even your death. They'll make you aware of the favorable times to push forward—whether or not the energy of the universe is supporting movement and growth—or when you need to remain still and be introspective. Should you start a project at a time when you're meant to slow down and look inward, you'll run into many obstacles and your plans will go awry. But if you start it at a time of growth—such as under the powerful number one, which represents the beginning of a cycle—the flow of energy is with you and you'll achieve long-term success.

When I perform a session for someone, I prefer to have his or her complete birth date, including the time that individual was born (if he or she happens to know it). And then, when I connect with the client intuitively, I feel as if an open book has fallen onto my lap that contains *all* of this person's information. Just as a doctor has medical records, I possess *life* records, which I can read instantaneously by speaking to the individual. This "file" contains information about the past and present, but also the future. In much the same way that science uses physical DNA, there exists an invisible DNA or code for one's life that reflects inner thoughts, actions, and outward behavior. In addition to "reading" someone, I also find it beneficial to use the tools of numerology and astrology in order to complement that which I already see.

One of the most fascinating things that happens during this process is that I'm able to detect clients' mental, physical, and spiritual health. I can actually help them overcome obstacles and transform their lives in a major way. I guide them to acknowledge who they are and where they need to go, and then their inner evolution can begin. Those individuals who have felt stuck in a behavior pattern for years can be put on the right track once they're made aware of the information that's available in the open book of the invisible world.

As you can see, using astrology and numerology helps you make decisions about the present and the future, but also make it easier for you to understand your connections to the larger whole. In particular, both of these systems help you decipher the current influences of the universe's energy upon your life.

You probably know your astrological sun sign—that is, your zodiac sign—but if you don't know your birth code, you can discover it by adding up the digits of your birth date. For example, March 3, 1968, would be $3 + 3 + 1 + 9 + 6 + 8 = 30$. This would then reduce to 3, because $3 + 0 = 3$ (note that the master numbers

11 and 22 do not get reduced). With so many threes in your code (your birth code, your birth month, and your day of birth), you'll experience the influence of 3 in your life quite strongly.

The reason these systems are tied into karmic resolution is because souls choose to be born at a certain time or in a particular year based on the issues they need to resolve. The soul calculates the perfect moment for entrance into the material world (which happens when a baby takes her first breath). The time and day when a baby is born is no coincidence; in fact, it's thoroughly predestined by the soul that has chosen to reincarnate.

When I was 18, a numerologist showed me how the numbers for the day I was born determined that I would do a great deal of caretaking for the sick in this lifetime. That's certainly not what I wanted to hear at that young age, and I didn't want to believe her, but it turned out to be true—this was my destiny, encoded by the calendar.

How to Recover and Reclaim Your Personal Past

When my mother was pregnant with me, she saw the opera *Carmen* and was mesmerized by the singer who played the title role of the gypsy girl. My mother vowed that if she gave birth to a girl, she would name her Carmen. When I was little, she'd tell me this story and insist that I looked just like the Carmen she'd seen at the opera. Did this happen because my mom had some awareness that I was destined to become a singer and to even be in operas someday? I believe she unknowingly accessed knowledge about my soul's past that was available in the invisible world.

I tapped into this knowledge as well. Despite my asthma as a child, I loved to sing and would tell everyone that I was going to be famous and perform on television. I won music contests and began taking opera lessons in my early teens, because I was certain that this was my destiny—I even had flashes from a past life of myself onstage. I ended up getting my first record deal at age 16 and sang pop and rock music on European television, but I always felt an affinity for opera.

Many people have long-buried memories of past lives that would give them clues to their hidden talents and destinies. Such memories may be activated by an image, touch, or sensation. If you think that you must have worked with animals in a previous life because you're practically obsessed with them, or you're drawn to French culture even though you have never visited the country and have no ties to it at all, your soul may be tugging at you to return to some of the interests and experiences of your past lives. The cyclical nature of time allows you to work through unresolved karma and enjoy the sacred connections you once had to certain people and the endeavors that gave you pleasure. The past will always be a part of who you are and remain with you through every incarnation.

I believe that hypnosis is a wonderfully effective technique for uncovering your forgotten personal past. It can help you cure bad habits and overcome phobias, in part because it allows your subconscious mind to retrieve memories that are at the root of these imbalances. For example, you may have been poor and gone hungry in a previous life, which causes you to overeat out of fear in this one. Or you might discover that an irrational behavior makes sense once you discover its origins in a past life and let go of the trauma that has lingered in your energy field.

Overall, I recommend hypnosis for past-life regression, even if you're simply seeking greater insight about yourself. After all, you could recover memories of talents that your conscious mind doesn't remember or find the courage to pursue your hidden passions now that they've been revealed.

Please know that contrary to what you see in the movies, hypnosis doesn't cause you to fall asleep. It puts you in a state of consciousness where you're aware of what's happening around you. No one can hypnotize you into doing something you truly don't want to do—not only will you know what you're doing, you'll remember what happened afterward. Even if you retrieve painful memories, a good hypnotist who is also a therapist can reassure you that you're okay, that what you're experiencing is merely a memory. In this way, you can bring to the surface karma that can be released at last.

• • •

Reminders of the karma we carry from lifetime to lifetime can be rather unsettling. Here's a story from my own life that proves this point.

During our life together, my husband had been an art dealer. It seemed to me that he found it necessary to bring home every other painting, vase, and ancient table he acquired, and our garage was filled to the ceiling with antique relics, including paintings from the 19th century.

Years before Virgil fell ill, I was woken from my sleep by a noise coming from the living room. I crept down the stairs and saw a pale, redheaded woman in a Victorian dress standing in my living room. I asked the beautiful spirit, "Who are you?"

She responded in a soft voice, "My name is Julia. I'm not going to let him stay with you. He was my husband, and he needs to come with me."

"Who?" I inquired, fearing her response.

The woman looked straight at me and answered: "Virgil." And with that, she vanished.

Several years later in the middle of the night, I was startled by the sound of Virgil grumbling in his sleep: "What do you want? No. Leave me alone, Julia." He then woke up immediately after saying those words.

"Who were you talking to?"

"This woman . . . Julia. I don't know who she is," he replied. "I have dreams about her from time to time. I don't understand. She always tells me to come to her."

I could feel the hairs on the back of my neck stand on end. "What does she look like?"

He took a moment and then replied, "She has red hair. And she's from a different time, with one of those long Victorian dresses."

About a month after my husband's passing, I was sorting through his hoard of antiques in the garage. I came upon a painting dating back to the 19th century that literally made me cry out. My daughter heard me and came running over to see what was going on. "What happened?" she asked. "I heard you scream."

"Look," I said, turning the picture over for her to see. She was as stunned as I was: in the painting was a man who had the same thick, dark hair, eyebrows, and mustache; full lips; and gleaming brown eyes as Virgil. If the portrait hadn't been created a hundred years before his birth, I would have sworn it was him. And next to the man in the painting was a pale, redheaded woman who looked exactly like Julia.

As you can see, our souls carry their memories from previous lives, and this impacts us in real ways in the present. Although we can only see the present, we limit our souls' complete experience by solely acknowledging the current incarnation.

In other words, if you think that this is the only life you have ever known, think again. At this very moment, you're in *one* phase of your soul's many cycles.

The Foundation for a Better Future

Because there's so much pain to be found in the past, we tend to forget the bleaker moments in history. As the saying goes, those who don't know their history are doomed to repeat it. Individually and collectively, we can break this cycle and heal our past; in so doing, we'll create a more positive present and future.

Every life event that happens to us—as well as every best-selling book that comes out and story that makes headlines in the media—has already been experienced by those who came before us. We're all a part of the collective human experience, and it's striking to see the similarities between the affairs of the ancient world and those of today.

To achieve balance in life, we have to spend time examining the past, imagining the future, and being present in our lives today. We have to go with the flow of our life cycles rather than trying to work according to our own timetables. We have to be aware of what we've done and what we're doing, in order to make conscious choices that lay the foundation for the future we hope to experience. By looking at history *and* paying attention to what might happen in the future, we get a better sense of the cycles affecting us.

Now, since conflict and resolving karma are a part of life, knowing the future won't allow you to avoid these elements, but it will let you prepare yourself for them emotionally and practically. For example, if a family reunion is set to take place at a time when you're meant to work through an issue, it's likely to be rockier than one held during a period when you're due to experience harmony. But this doesn't mean that you should avoid the gathering—just know what you're getting into and welcome it as an opportunity to make real progress toward healing. Pray for wisdom, insight, and patience as you enter into any situation that you know will be challenging.

You can also build upon the foundation you've laid for the future you'd like to experience. In addition to helping you retrieve memories, hypnosis performed by a skilled professional can instill in you new beliefs that you'd like to hold on to, such as *I can't stand the taste or smell of cigarettes,* or *I feel beautiful in my body and experience joy whenever I see my reflection in the mirror.* You can choose which beliefs you'd like to adopt. The powerful technique of hypnosis allows you to take the new beliefs you'd like to have and turn them into memories in your brain. So you'll be able to say no to cigarettes, or yes to your self-image, and this will feel natural. In a sense, you will have brought what you want to happen into the present.

Remember how I said that in the invisible world the future affects our lives today? Well, a vision of a better future creates a reality that is more likely to manifest because you've created it. You actually bring it into your world and make it real in the material realm. You do the same if you project a negative future by worrying and imagining the worst. Have you ever said, "I knew this relationship wouldn't work out!" "I have bad luck with women," or something similar? Is it possible that you created that future and brought it into your life?

Visualizations, affirmations, and working with *dream boards*— where you draw or paste pictures of what you'd like to achieve onto a poster you look at every day—all create a powerful intention that affects you in the present. When you imagine the future, you take one potential outcome from the field of possibilities in the invisible world and give it life in the present by believing in it. By doing so, you make a more probable future.

Praying to the Divine helps you acknowledge what it is that you want to generate and draw in support for. However, to bring about what you desire, you must also act. Take the necessary steps toward manifesting this vision, and work hard at achieving it.

Whenever you set your intention for creating a particular set of circumstances, remember that you're not the only one who's influencing them. Everyone on the planet is interconnected, and their actions and beliefs today affect what will happen tomorrow. Be open to whatever comes your way—you might not have yet imagined what will bring you great joy.

Predictions and Prophecies

Predictions can give birth to a dream and open the door to new possibilities. Yet people are often surprised when I tell them a vision of what they can anticipate down the road, because fate takes unexpected turns. For example, I've had clients insist they couldn't get pregnant, but I saw that they *would* have a child—and they did! And other clients have told me that they didn't think they'd ever find love again, but I foresaw the romantic partner who would come into their lives, his or her initials or name, and even where the introductory encounters would take place. But none of that happens without someone taking action.

Then there was Virginia, who was in despair because her home was in foreclosure. I told her that she was meant to be there, the paperwork would support this choice, and she should stay put. For nearly two years, she and her family remained in their house without paying toward the mortgage, while she fought for what was theirs.

Finally, Virginia became so scared that her family would be evicted that she ignored my advice and moved everyone to an apartment. Most of her belongings went into a storage facility, and she began to run ads to sell her furniture, her treasured grand piano, and other items. To her dismay, and despite her rock-bottom prices, *nothing* sold. I reiterated to her that this was because she was not meant to leave that home. The future, in which she was living in her house, was affecting her present and ensuring that not a single chair or end table sold.

Shortly afterward, Virginia drove by the house and saw that it was still empty, with no FOR SALE sign in the front yard. Bolstered by my prediction, she moved her entire family and all their furniture back in and continued the legal battle! In the end, the lending company was never able to prove that it owned the mortgage, so Virginia eventually gained possession of the home she was supposed to live in.

What an intuitive sees is only one possible outcome, of course, since your free will may bring about something very different. However, if you're willing to glimpse what could be, your mind may open to a future you never dared to dream for yourself.

• • •

It's too bad that human beings have clung to the idea of a doomsday for thousands of years, even though such prophecies and other negative forecasts are just reflections of our fears. The moment of the supposed apocalypse comes, nothing happens, and then everyone forgets how they got swept up in collective fear and starts worrying about the next one. For example, many people were terrified about the bug that was supposed to affect our computers and lead to mass chaos on January 1, 2000. No major catastrophes occurred, due in part to the fact that we acknowledged the potential problems and assertively addressed the situation to prevent them. Now someone has set December 21, 2012, as the new date. But believe me, that day will be uneventful, too. It will simply be a turning point, not a dramatic shift that creates dreadful events.

I often wonder why seers in the past never seemed to envision anything positive. Where was the prediction for the end of slavery or the invention of antibiotics? I don't know of any prophet throughout history who envisioned that humans would walk on the moon or communicate with others around the globe in real time as we can now. Instead, they anticipated world wars and deaths of leaders.

The negative tone of predictions throughout history is due to our being programmed to dread difference and suffering. Yet we can make the choice to let these dire prophecies influence us positively by heeding their warnings and changing our behavior. And we've certainly woken up before: the fact that we've had the capability to destroy all life on the planet for decades with nuclear weapons hasn't led to another world war; instead, it's brought us to a deeper understanding of our responsibility to find common ground and create peace and understanding.

Seeing something negative in the future should simply serve as an impetus to modify what we're doing today, for we have the ability to correct our trajectory. We must remember that this world was originally a paradise that was created for us to enjoy—we need to stop imagining all the horrors that we might create and instead begin projecting a positive future.

As an intuitive, I do see positive events happening in the lives of individuals, and I feel strongly that humanity is going to come out of this turbulent time having learned great lessons. We're absolutely going to enter a new era of peace and higher consciousness, but we need to stop worrying and get to work directing the forces of change so that they work in our favor. Then we can know for sure that our future is destined to be brighter.

Honoring Those Who Came Before and Those Yet to Come

You are linked to every soul in this universe, from the first human who walked upon the earth to the last person who will breathe in its air. Certainly, you feel more of a bond to your parents, siblings, or friends than to a tribesman who lived on the other side of the globe a thousand years ago or to a person who is yet to be born. Yet remember that time is infinite—and the past, present, and future all exist as possibilities in the invisible world—so you *are* actually just as connected with those you love as with your ancestors and the generations who are yet to come.

To end the divisiveness and strife on the planet, it's essential that we recognize these sacred connections that exist beyond time, geographical boundaries, and all of the other limitations we've invented to organize the tangible world. Now that we know we're related beyond religion, ethnic group, or gender, our challenge is to stop making so much of our differences and balance what we understand about each other.

We don't know what future generations will hold, if they'll be shocked by some of the choices we made or amused by what we believed. What we do know is that we have the same responsibility toward future generations that those who came before us had: collectively and as individuals, all of us must do our part to keep the world a healthy, safe place. Parents do this instinctively for their offspring, but we all have this duty to everyone who will come after us. We have to aim for an ideal world for each and every child of this planet, even if we don't completely succeed at creating that legacy. To embrace wholeliness is to renew our faith in the good of humanity and recognize that all souls are worth our efforts at progress and positive change.

We're also accountable to those who have been here before us, no matter if they lived 2 years ago or 2,000 years ago. "Respect your elders," we often say, and this should extend to everyone who's lived throughout the course of time. We respect them by learning from them, which requires us to look back to what we've forgotten or brushed aside, and we can learn from the mistakes of the past and resolve the karma we've inherited. We're obliged to look back so that we can look forward into a better future.

You may be disconnected from your lineage, but you have the ability to reclaim those connections. Let's say that you're adopted and your ethnicity is African American, but you have a strong affinity to Japanese culture. Embrace that. You *do* have a link to all people everywhere, and perhaps in a past life you lived in Japan or are meant to live there presently. Don't let your limited no-tions about who you are and where you belong prevent you from exploring all the many futures that might await you.

In your many incarnations, you've probably been male and female, rich and poor, Asian and American. Again, it may be that despite having been raised in Los Angeles, events that occurred in a previous life in Japan are calling to you. Or perhaps it's the future that's beckoning you—it could be that it's your destiny to meet someone in Japan whom you have unresolved karma with, and the two of you will work through it together.

As you open yourself up to all of your sacred connections and recognize the complexity of how time works in the invisible realm, you'll start to have a better understanding of your responsibility for resolving karma. Ask for help from the Divine, and don't turn away from the synchronicities that Spirit has orchestrated on your behalf. Learn from your past, envision your future, and marvel at the many ways in which you're able to work with the flow of time to assist your return to wholeliness.

How to Get into Sync with the Rhythms of Time

Observe

When you picture what your life will be in the future, is it negative? How much time do you spend imagining what you might create and how you might contribute to the world?

If you don't know what you want, think about what you value. Picture what your day would be like if you had what you desire most. Imagine what the news headlines would be. Observe how it feels as you visualize this better world for yourself.

Now look back to your history and ask yourself what lessons can be learned from it. Psychological counseling is a wonderful tool for gaining valuable information from your past because an objective observer can help you be honest about what you've experienced and the choices you've made—and assist you in letting go of your shame, anger, or sadness. You must forgive yourself for mistakes you've made so that you can take something positive away from what happened.

Also, notice the people and places you're drawn to. Pay close attention to so-called coincidences that may alert you to a life cycle that will help you face, and resolve, your karma.

Once you've had a chance to think about what you want for the future (perhaps by looking at the significance of what's happened in your past), take some time to get these thoughts down in your journal.

Pray

Pray for support in healing the past—yours and that of your group. Request the strength that's necessary to let go of your ego's resistance. You may not be responsible for what your countrymen or members of your religious group did years ago, but you are here today living with the results of their actions, and you can choose to help heal those who were hurt. Your ancestors wish to resolve any bad karma they created, so assist them. Ask them and the Divine for guidance so that you'll know how to heal the whole.

Pray for a better future. Ask for guidance on how to create the best possible future for all. And pray to recognize the cycles of your life and imagine better days when your situation seems grim. Ask that Spirit send you signs that you'll be okay, that you'll receive a glimpse of what this better future might look like. Then pay close attention to your dreams—or to any situations, people, or events you feel inexplicably drawn toward. The Divine sends symbolic messages and prods you by attracting you to that which you are meant to experience.

Act

Create a dream board. Use poster board, photographs, or your computer's software to place pictures and words on a background . . . and create a visual representation of the future you envision. Each day, spend some time looking at the board and allow your heart to feel enthusiasm, hope, contentment, and any other positive emotion that comes up as a result of viewing the images and words that encapsulate your ideal future.

Explore your past so that you may more compassionately view yourself and others who may have hurt you long ago. Research your family, religion, and country. Read a history book or watch a documentary. Interview your older relatives, including your parents, about what their lives were like when you were young or they were growing up. Truly listen, and then ponder how people who influenced you thought, perceived, and felt. Take in this information, even if it stirs up embarrassment, sadness, frustration, or anger. It's important to know your history so that you can express love toward all those, including yourself, who made mistakes out of fear or ignorance. By viewing the past with an attitude of love and forgiveness, you bring peace and power into your life today.

Although it's likely to be difficult for your rational mind to comprehend and accept that you can heal the past and bring a better future into your life today, this power *can* be yours. As you claim it, you'll find that you're ready to acknowledge and understand the limitations of religious and scientific teachings that you've been told are the best ways to make sense of your experiences.

Both entities can *help* you comprehend the material world and your experiences in it, but ultimately they are distorted lenses that prevent you from seeing clearly and experiencing wholeliness, the totality of the invisible and visible worlds. Whenever there's a contradiction between this world and the realm beyond the senses, remember that the unseen reality supersedes this one.

Religious teachings are inadequate ways of encapsulating the lessons of the invisible world, and scientific teachings don't do justice to the nature of our existence. Fortunately, once you recognize how limiting these two lenses of perception are, you'll free yourself to know and fully experience your true spiritual nature, which is wholeliness. Then it will be far easier to bring it into your everyday interactions, conversations, actions, and relationships (which you'll learn about in Part IV).

CHAPTER

9

A NEW VIEW OF RELIGION, SCIENCE, AND SPIRITUALITY

"What is arising now is not a new belief system, a new religion, spiritual ideology or mythology. We are coming to the end not only of mythologies but also of ideologies and belief systems."

— ECKHART TOLLE

All religions promote core universal values of showing compassion toward our neighbors, treating others as we'd like to be treated, and expressing our love and respect for the Divine. *Religion* comes from the Latin verb *religare,* meaning "to restrain or tie back." The word, therefore, connotes the rejoining of human being to Spirit, and also the reunion of humans with each other under one universal belief.

Yet all too often, people have used religion as an excuse for being divisive. Group ego gets in the way, and individuals focus on perceived differences. They point to the holy writings of another group that have been taken out of context and say, "You see? Those people aren't like us." Too many religious leaders preach, "Ours is the best, the true religion, and God favors us." These divisions have led to the suffering and even deaths of millions, and the wholeliness of worshipping God has been forsaken.

In this time of great transformation, we're shifting out of our low-consciousness ideas. America, in particular, is becoming a spiritual nation rather than a religious one. Our younger generations are wisely recognizing that even though there are many belief systems, there's only one Divine Force and no "right" religion. Soon, we'll come together globally as we never have before and balance our personal religious beliefs with our spiritual nature, which connects us to everyone and everything.

We'll also come to see science, which many have made the primary system for understanding our lives, as simply one lens to view the world through. Then we'll end this ridiculous argument that pits it against religion. We'll respect what physical data and research can teach us, but recognize their limitations: they largely ignore the existence of the invisible world that determines our experiences in the visible world. The gaping rifts between religion, spirituality, and science—and the divisions between people—will heal as we embrace wholeliness.

All Is United Under One Divine Love

Many practitioners of Christianity, Islam, and Judaism still see God as separate from man, and their leaders teach that we must approach the Divine with intercessory prayers. Followers are taught that this God dwells in the heavens, apart from His creation. From His seat on high, removed from us, He judges and punishes, operating from His own mysterious sense of justice that's beyond our understanding. At the same time, this Supreme Being is said to have the power to show mercy, bestow grace, answer prayers, and perform miracles . . . so we're told to appeal to Him for intervention.

For many people, such a view of the Divine has provided comfort and a sense of peace—but for others, this perception of the nature of God and our interactions with Him have led to fear, sadness, and anger. These individuals find such a narrow understanding of a Higher Power to be insufficient to answer our questions regarding the sacred complexities of life; more explicitly, they feel that religion often fails to fulfill us.

Fortunately, you can open up to a new understanding of Spirit, the Source of all love, healing, and harmony. If you accept that wholeliness is your true nature, you form a very different relationship with the Divine. You will recognize that the Creator, just like you, is a conscious force, and anything separate from this force and wisdom is an illusion. All is unified in the great consciousness (which has also been called the *unified field*), but this can be very difficult for you to perceive as long as you're in human form.

Everything in the universe is made up of energy that has consciousness. Evidence of this is everywhere we turn: in the perfectly structured orbit of every object in our galaxy, in the intelligence of every creature to satisfy its Divinely inspired purpose on Earth, and in the symbiotic relationship between all living organisms. You and Spirit are one, sharing a brilliant consciousness with all of the creatures and beings in existence.

The Divine is your supreme Source of love, power, wisdom, and abundance—like a river flowing throughout the entire universe, it is always available to nourish you. However, if you fear God's wrath (something even nonbelievers experience when they're afraid of death or suffering), this will blind you to your nature as a conscious being who is, was, and forever will be connected to this Higher Power.

Every religion offers variants on the truth of the Divine. If you were to study the teachings of different faiths, you'd discover many distinct ideas about God. You'd also see that humans tend to cast Spirit in their own image: The ancient Greeks and Romans conceived of gods and goddesses who exhibited all the character flaws of human beings. Ancient peoples in Scandinavia and Egypt also believed in many gods, and if you were to look at what those beings represented, you'd see that each one embodied a limited number of aspects of the complex, sacred force.

By studying other beliefs, you might be very surprised to discover that those that seem dissimilar have much more in common than you thought. The narratives of almost all of the world's religions overlap in that they each speak of one Divine Creator who created all life on Earth. In the Christian, Jewish, and Muslim faiths, God is that Supreme Being who said "Be"; and in response, all things came into existence. In Hinduism, Lord Brahma is responsible for all that exists. In the creation story believed by the Australian Aborigines, Baiame, the maker of many things, placed humans on Earth. And the Chinese creation story, which attributes life to the yin and yang, teaches that everything was formed purposely by sacred forces.

While our minds aren't able to fully comprehend the Divine Force, we can understand and accept this truth that is a part of every modern and ancient religion: the nature of Spirit is goodness and love.

• • •

As a child, I was taught the same religious concepts and doctrines that my parents and grandparents had learned. The vast majority of us were (and still are) traditional Orthodox believers. Our churches were adorned with icons, the bearded priests wore their ceremonial robes, everyone attended church on Sunday to listen to the weekly sermon . . . and this was all we knew or cared to know. We simply stuck to tradition and challenged nothing that was fed to us. There was really no such thing as changing one's religion, studying spirituality, or becoming an atheist. Under the rule of our old government regime, church attendance was not obligatory. Despite this relative freedom, it seemed that no one felt compelled to question his or her beliefs, indulge a healthy sense of curiosity, or explore other options regarding Divine teachings.

Therefore, when I came to America, I was shocked to find people of all religions—and even those who rejected religion altogether—living in one place. My connection to the Divine then took on new meaning, as I realized that neither I nor the person next to me who believed something totally different was right or wrong. Naturally, I started questioning everything that I'd been taught, but never disavowing it. I tried to figure out what seemed most plausible to me and what could bring peace to all children of the Divine. It seemed right that we should all believe in some universal Force who watches over us and cares for us, as most religions teach. Thus, what I came up with was this concept of wholeliness, the one belief that unites us all under one Divine love.

Why has religion been so divisive? Medicine men, shamans, priests, saints, and spiritual leaders have given us wise teachings about our spiritual nature and relationship to the Divine, but we've forgotten them. Religion, and later science, distracted us from the truth, and we began to feel cut off and frightened. We can forgo the unhealthy restrictions that we've placed on our connection to Spirit and reclaim the wholeliness that's been lost.

Atheism and Fundamentalism

Religion and spiritual beliefs have been a part of human cultures around the globe for thousands of years. Since humankind first developed the ability to reason, we've attributed our own existence to a higher being. Today, however, an increasing number of people are identifying themselves as nonreligious or even as atheists. Atheism was not commonly discussed or accepted for much of our history, but in the 19th century, philosophers like Karl Marx (who famously disdained religion as "the opiate of the masses"), Friedrich Engels, and Friedrich Nietzsche brought it some notoriety.

When atheistic Communism took hold in China and the U.S.S.R., it was in part due to the corruption of churches, which over hundreds of years had become too concerned with power in the visible world. Many turned against religion because they saw how it had been used to justify oppression, divisiveness, and violence. In short, by exploiting their power, a handful of authorities sadly ruined the prospect of a Divine relationship for millions of people.

Too often, atheists disdain religion as something only foolish, unintelligent people subscribe to. Those who hold on to this belief do so because it gives them a false sense of certainty: they believe that science can provide all the answers, while faith in a Higher Power holds people back from wisdom. Given the excesses of many religious people and institutions, this point of view is understandable.

However, if atheists were to let go of any personal feelings about having been pressured or persecuted by individuals claiming to act in God's name, they might see that atheism and fundamentalism are actually quite similar: Both reject the beauty of mystery and cling to the false security of having all the answers. Atheists assert that human beings will understand all the workings of the universe through science, while fundamentalists insist that their holy books and sacred teachings explain everything that's worth discussing or knowing about. As with any extreme in life, both of these mentalities lead to imbalance and away from wholeliness.

Even as more individuals are admitting that they don't believe in a Supreme Being, we're also seeing a rise in fundamentalism. This isn't a lasting trend, but more like a last gasp coming from those who are terrified by the uncertainty of humanity's direction. The more that people feel insecure about what's ahead, the more we see them cling to whatever promises their safety. But fundamentalism will ultimately fade as we find comfort in wholeliness.

• • •

Most individuals fall somewhere in between the two extremes of being absolutely positive that there is no God and absolutely positive that what they've been taught about the Divine is correct and everything else is a lie. The rigid positions of atheism or fundamentalism provide a sense of comfort to some, particularly in uncertain times. Yet both philosophies ultimately take their followers away from the real power that would sustain us through difficulties: the perception of humans as spiritual beings interwoven with the larger whole of reality that's mysterious, beautiful, and sacred.

I once worked with a client named Mary who called me from overseas. Mary was a devout Christian who read the Bible word for word and regularly sought out her priest for guidance. She stated firmly that she believed in nothing relating to psychics or medium-ship, and that her religion absolutely forbade such nonsense. And yet she felt compelled to speak to me despite her position that the work I do is "evil and not of God."

Mary told me that her 28-year-old son had been killed in a car accident, and she had such a powerful need to communicate with him and feel his loving presence once more that she was willing to go against her faith for the first time in her life. When I began to describe to her how, at the time of the accident, her son had lost the cross he wore around his neck every day, Mary began to cry. I also told her that he'd left behind a newborn child who had *G* as an initial; the specifics of his injuries; who had caused the acci-dent; and even that her son's grandmother, who had passed away two years prior, was waiting for him on the other side.

Through tears, Mary validated that the information I gave her was true. She said that she had no idea how I knew all of these things, but I'd awakened her to a world of new possibilities. By the end of our session, she confessed to me that our conversa-tion was the most blessed experience she had ever lived through. Mary wholeheartedly thanked me for helping her cope with every mother's worst nightmare. She admitted that no member of her church had ever been able to offer her the peace she found through mediumship. And she wondered how something that offers such comfort to people could be due to anything other than the work of an all-loving, compassionate God.

What about the Paranormal?

Ancient people who possessed the power to communicate with the Divine were greatly respected in society, and leaders reg-ularly consulted seers and mediums to help them access the invis-ible world. We forgot the value of this wisdom as science began explaining what religion, mediumship, and the like could not.

Yet while science focuses on the mysteries of the visible world and religion tries to make sense of the mysteries of the invisible world, each is looking at half of the picture instead of the whole.

As Einstein once said, "Science without religion is lame; religion without science is blind."

In order to prevent science and technology from being used in destructive ways, we need spiritual awareness and sensitivity to human life. We may have figured out how to split the atom, but we've forgotten how to interact with the Sacred Force of the invisible world that guides us toward ethical behavior. Within the framework of science and religion, the credibility of one must never outweigh the other.

This shift from a spiritual explanation of our existence to an objective one has been evident over the last few hundred years, as we've made remarkable advances in the medical and scientific fields, and atheism and agnosticism have increased in popularity. While we should take pride in our advancements in science, we shouldn't dismiss what are called *paranormal experiences*. The prefix *para* means "beyond," but I would argue that these phenomena are perfectly normal. We also have no reason to fear or dismiss the *occult* (*occultus* in Latin simply means "hidden"); certainly, the workings of the invisible world are often hidden from the senses.

Even today, many people insist that we can't communicate with the invisible world. Religion often sees mediumship as a dark art that is to be feared, while those with scientific minds see it as a false art that defies logic. Interestingly, they choose to ignore the new theories in quantum physics that shed light on these experiences, such as the butterfly effect and Bell's theorem. (Very simply, Bell's theorem states that whatever you do to one particle will affect another particle miles away if those two particles were once connected, and they must have an invisible way of communicating instantly so that one can have an empathetic response to the other.)

The Divine and the paranormal are forever present and limitless, while our information and perceptions are finite and narrow. I believe that as humanity undergoes the impending shift in consciousness, we'll regain trust in Spirit and renew our respect for the mysterious workings of the invisible world.

I also believe that the fear of what can't be explained by priests, holy books, and traditional theology will begin to fade. As we embrace our connections to the Divine, the spirits who watch over us, and each other, we'll realize that religion falls short of the experience of wholeliness, which can't be fully captured in words or teachings.

As soon as you try to depict God, you limit your perception of Him (which is why some religions have edicts against painting or drawing Divine images, and other religions insist that you must not say or write His name; unfortunately, these teachings have been taken too literally, and the original meanings have been forgotten).

Whether you perceive Spirit as a loving Father, Mother, or nurturing Force with no gender certainly doesn't matter. Whenever you invoke the Divine Force using words, or you imagine whom you are praying to, recognize that your mind can't possibly apprehend such vastness and complexity, and that's okay. What's important is not that you "get it right," because there is no right way to talk to God or connect with His love. Just be sure that the words you use, the rituals you perform, and the images you envision help you experience wholeliness.

As we get past the religious teachings that divide us from others or make us feel separate from Spirit, we'll see more acknowledgment of paranormal experiences. Increasingly, humans will believe that they can directly communicate with the Divine and the spirits on the other side, and receive answers in the form of inner knowing, symbolic messages, and synchronicities. The recognition of our ability to participate in dialogue with the invisible world will become one of the most beautiful advancements of humankind.

Wholeliness, Science, and Religion

It's interesting—and not by chance—that within both scientific and religious beliefs, we see evidence of wholeliness. Scientists recognize the relationships between entities that seem to be separate, while they're also aware of the diversity of life. They strive to find a unified theory, such as string theory, that can explain how everything in the universe works together—because, like all humans, they have an inner yearning for harmony. Whichever way you look at it, none of us can escape our desire for unity. Deep down, we all need to understand our connections, but what's most important is to trust in them and their power to help us heal and feel loved and safe.

Even the theory of evolution can be seen as an explanation of how we are all one: every creature on this earth evolved from one that came before it, going all the way back to the first single-celled organism that existed billions of years ago. For example, our genes act as physical evidence that ties us to our common ancestors, and we share 96 percent of our DNA with chimpanzees. Although we look very different from birds, which look very different from insects, evolution has validated the fact that we all derive from one common source, one common history. We see the differences in skin color and hair texture between one person and another, but what we don't see is the incredible similarities we all share right down to our DNA.

Noted physicist Stephen Hawking claims that there's no need for an intelligent, supreme being to set the forces of the universe in motion. He, like many scientists, believes that life and death simply happen, and that mathematics, chance, and probability can explain all natural phenomena. This mechanistic viewpoint is in opposition to wholeliness—although it acknowledges the forces of energy in the universe, it dismisses the patterns that give us a glimpse of the perfection of creation, as well as our sacred connections when we access the invisible world. It also assumes that there's no purpose to life and no consciousness orchestrating the exquisite harmony of the natural world and the heavens. At this point, my hope is that you, dear reader, have begun to scrutinize your consciousness and the meaning of existence, and therefore also question this limited perspective.

• • •

Even as scientists continue to learn more, they come across more mysteries! They have to deal with the fact that some of the ideas that are part of spiritual traditions, such as the mind-body-spirit connection, have validity. These days, quantum mechanics and quantum physics are supplying the link that unites the invisible and visible worlds. At every level of reality, we're recognizing that the old cause-and-effect rules and mathematical formulas can't explain natural phenomena. Scientists can't account for the instant, empathetic response one particle has when another one that it was once unified with is altered, but metaphysics tells us that this is due to the interconnectedness of all things.

Everything on this planet is part of the fabric of reality that operates according to rules scientists and mathematicians are still puzzling over. Intuitive people may not understand the complexities of how immediate, invisible transfer of information happens, but they recognize that it occurs all the time. For example, a mother knows when her child who's away at college is ill because of their intrinsic connection. A person notices when something is wrong with his best friend, even if he can't put his finger on exactly which comment set off alarm bells during a phone conversation.

Metaphysics incorporates ideas from science, along with the wisdom of the ancients (who believed in the invisible world) and all that we experience in the present. It aims to draw a picture of a complex yet harmonious universe that is interconnected in ways we can't always understand. What medicine men and spiritual teachers have taught for thousands of years won't be so casually dismissed by scientists in the future thanks to the discoveries of quantum physics. I believe that someday we'll have machines that actually prove the presence of spirits interacting in the visible world. There will even be machines that act as mediums, allowing us to communicate with those who have passed.

We don't need to reject fact or logic—we simply need to expand objective knowledge and balance it with other ways of understanding the human experience. We must realize that science is only one truth within a world that's full of them.

At the same time, within the sacred texts that religions have been built upon, lie hints of our ancestors' awareness of wholeliness. Ancient narratives carry the wisdom of how we all share a history and came from one source; they also share how we became integrated into the whole of creation in relationship to the planet, the Divine, and each other. They've revealed the unity of all souls with Spirit.

Unfortunately, when it comes to religion, we've let our overly literal interpretations of ancient teachings divide us. We've made a mockery of the original, inspirational intent of sacred writings. Those who teach that the Bible contradicts science, and that we should therefore believe that the earth is 6,000 years old, are thinking in a very limited way. The Bible, like all holy books, uses metaphors to convey profound ideas . . . and because human beings with agendas have tinkered with it, it is flawed.

The words that we read in the Bible today have been filtered by influential people who sought power or let their egos get the better of them—they took out or added certain passages, or misconstrued them in ways that validated their fear. For example, King James deliberately requested that those translating his version of the Bible glorify any leader in order to furtively influence readers to see *him* as chosen by God to rule over them. And the lost books of the Bible, known as the Apocrypha, were never actually lost; rather, they were deemed unsuitable and banned. As the Bible was being copied by hand over and over again, scribes made mistakes here and there, replaced certain words, and might have added a verse or two to "improve" it.

Know that *all* holy books have been influenced by mere men to varying degrees. Often, they have been translated from one language to another at least once, and the meanings of certain words have evolved over the course of time. Stories taken out of context of their original cultures can also easily be misinterpreted. Whenever you read holy texts, don't take them literally; rather, look at the *heart* of the teachings. By doing so, you'll see the connections between many belief systems (because ultimately, all religions are rooted in wholeliness).

Religion vs. Spirituality

Clearly, religion involves interpretation. Spirituality, on the other hand, involves *experience*—it's the search for meaning and the longing to be a part of something larger than oneself. Spirituality is a yearning that's satisfied when we experience the presence of the Divine; in a sense, it is the craving for wholeliness on Earth.

The problem is that we took the focus off of the spiritual experience—wholeliness—and put it on the interpretation. Today, religion is often wrapped up in our cultural identity; for example, we say "I'm an Irish Catholic," "I'm a Jewish New Yorker," or "I'm a European Christian." We don't necessarily realize that our faith and cultural identity can be balanced with our identity as part of the larger whole. Both descriptions can coexist peacefully within our hearts.

Once a person has experienced unification with all creation, she awakens to her spiritual nature and feels loved and supported, powerful and at peace forever. Her heart opens to the beauty and perfection of the invisible world, and she feels a desire to bring those qualities to life so that everyone can experience them.

Religion is the result of the desire to understand and express the power of wholeliness, as the human mind wants to explain spiritual beliefs and observations about our nature. Ancient people created religions using imagery, stories, and rituals in the hopes that they could better comprehend the inexplicable workings of the world.

Personal beliefs tend to provide us with strength and comfort, while religious rituals can help us enforce our relationship with Spirit and enhance our spiritual nature. And when it comes to others, we can appreciate the beauty of their own Divine expressions without being suspicious or judgmental. We can see religion as a tool for understanding and experiencing our sacred, healing connections.

Religion and spirituality have been out of balance for too long. We can help bring them back into harmony by challenging our churches and religious communities to be what they were meant to be: centers of spirituality and community life, where our spiritual nature is nurtured and we're inspired to act upon our values to heal the world. We can stop placing so much importance on religious dogma and convincing our neighbor to adopt our ideas about God. We can instead simply try to manifest wholeliness so that we may all know Divine grace.

You can bring yourself back from the bias of religion by shifting your consciousness to let yourself feel, at least for a short while, a sense of spiritual elevation, personal symmetry, and joy. This can come about while communicating with the Divine through prayer or meditation, or when quietly contemplating wholeliness or expressing your beliefs through action. At these times, Spirit's sacred presence will gently blanket you in reassurance, lovingly caress your soul, and satiate you with a sense of total peace.

Have you ever sat admiring the beauty of a brilliantly sunny day and inhaled a deep breath of contentment, or witnessed winter's first snowfall coating the roofs of houses with its white splendor, and noticed warmth stirring within your heart? You may have felt this moment of fulfillment while watching your children play, cuddling with your pet, or laughing at one of the absurdities of life with a good friend. These moments may be fleeting, but they offer a brief glimpse of wholeliness that reminds you that separateness and disconnection are illusions of the visible world. These are the times when you experience the perfection of creation.

You can reach this euphoric state of being more often, and for more than a few seconds, before being drawn back to earthly dullness. Slow down and simply take in the elegance of the world, the interactions of people, and the universal behaviors of nature. Express love, shun anger, be patient, and listen with compassion. Act respectfully toward yourself and all creatures. Treat the earth as your precious home. Most of all, believe in sacred connections, and then you will experience them.

Remain cognizant of how grateful you are for the activities you enjoy, the blissful circumstances in life, and the people who support and love you. The next time you feel a sense of gratitude toward the Divine, say a simple prayer of thanks. Open your awareness to the perfection of creation in even small moments, and you'll find that your entire body feels different as your vibration rises. This is wholeliness.

• • •

While many people may call themselves "nonreligious," it doesn't mean that they don't believe in God. They simply don't subscribe to the rigid dogma and theology of religion. They may also be uncomfortable with expressing their faith in the traditional way of belonging to an organization and performing strict rituals. For them, it's important to separate the traditional notion of religion or God from the grander unity of wholeliness. Unfortunately, fear can hold them back from acknowledging the empowering connections they have to a larger whole.

Although the numbers of spiritual explorers (those who are more focused on compassion and love than theology) may seem small in comparison to the throngs who identify with particular religions, this group *is* steadily growing. In fact, we're currently headed away from the dominance of religion and toward balanced spirituality. More churches will even embrace wholeliness and unity as individuals move forward on their sacred journeys, unafraid to defy traditional teachings and established leaders.

If you happen to be looking for an organization where you can feel supported in your spiritual exploration, you might look into attending the services at New Thought churches such as Unity Church and the Church of Religious Science, as well as Unitarian Universalist churches. You may also decide to forgo the more structured experience altogether and instead find spiritual support within the larger community. Or perhaps you'll find comfort in the church of your childhood, discovering deeper meanings in its teachings now that you're a mature adult. Familiar prayers will mean so much more once you've embraced wholeliness, because you'll go beyond the words and understand their universality. After all, don't we all pray for the same things? Don't we desire to express the joys of experiencing our connection to the force of love?

As more and more of us come into balance, the rifts between science and religion are going to be mended. We're all coming closer together on the common ground of spirituality.

How to Balance Religion and Spirituality

Observe

Identify your personal religious and spiritual beliefs, and contemplate their origins. For instance, did you learn them in childhood, did you develop them later as a result of your own spiritual journey, or was it a combination of both? If you don't have a particular faith, think about what your beliefs are, as well as what you think about the nature of suffering and the human experience. As you look at the origins of your opinions, ask yourself, "If I'd been exposed to different circumstances, would I still hold these beliefs? How firmly do I hold them? What might change them?" If it feels frightening to examine these topics, explore that, too. Consider whether there's a religion or spiritual tradition that intrigues you more than your own, and why that is.

If you have the chance to attend a service of a different faith or listen to someone describe his methods of worship, simply observe without judgment. Become curious about the faith's origins and how it may help people cope with the difficulties of life and find peace. Notice similarities between your spiritual beliefs and those that underlie the credo of this particular religion.

Pay close attention to how you feel if you decide to go to an unfamiliar house of worship. What sort of sentiments fill your spirit, and what thoughts cross your mind? Do you feel comfortable and welcome at the service? Do the words of the minister, rabbi, or speaker resonate internally for you? Do the words emotionally or spiritually engage you?

Exposing yourself to spiritual principles that you know little about can be a very powerful experience. However you decide to do so, make sure you take the time to write about your reactions, reflections, and emotions in your journal.

Pray

Pray with others. You might start or join a group that meets at a designated time and place to pray for specific people, personal enlightenment, the well-being of humanity, or whatever is important to its members. Invite individuals of different religions and traditions to participate.

I believe that it's more powerful if you can unite with others in their intentions and find the beauty and sacredness in their words as you communicate with God. You can all say prayers in unison or recite them silently if anyone is uncomfortable using the prayers of other religions.

If you're the one who's fearful of using the terms and images from other faiths, explore why that is. (Rest assured that the Divine will never get upset with you for opening your heart and mind to discover the scope of someone else's beliefs.)

You might also simultaneously pray with others around the world. Groups like Call to Conscious Evolution (**www.calltoconsciousevolution.org**) ask people to pray for specific outcomes at a designated time. When many do so in unison, the effects on the world are powerful.

Act

After observing a different religion's practices or attending an interfaith ceremony, introduce yourself to other attendees and find out what you have in common. If you can, join a discussion group committed to exploring spiritual beliefs or understanding other faiths. Read about other religions, and spend time with people who belong to them—or who have no religion at all. Listen to these individuals when they talk about their values and ideas, and engage in respectful discussions with them.

The old adage "Don't discuss religion or politics" assumes that we don't have enough love and courage to have productive, thoughtful, and respectful conversations that lead to greater wisdom. I think we need to have more faith in ourselves; and besides, we must challenge each other to learn to discuss the most important, heartfelt topics in a loving way. If we refrain from conversing with others regarding their personal beliefs, how will we ever broaden our perspective of the world?

When you embrace wholeliness and commit yourself to creating harmony and healing in the world, you can participate in positive discourse on these topics, because you're willing to set aside your ego and learn. As Socrates so correctly established, only through dialogue can we reach the ultimate truth.

When you balance religion and spirituality, you will find that science is a useful tool for understanding the visible world and won't feel threatened or upset if it seems to contradict religious teachings. You'll remember that spirituality and wholeliness involve surpassing literalism to recognize the beauty and mystery of the spiritual realm and the perfection of its expression. You'll be able to appreciate the poetry of how holy texts describe this world without feeling that you must reject scientific evidence and theories, and you'll actually enjoy pondering the mysterious interaction of the invisible and visible worlds.

Having changed on the inside, you'll now be able to see how to shift your thoughts and behaviors. It will be easier to open your mind to new ways of thinking, because until now, you've been looking at life through a narrow lens that doesn't capture the complete landscape of people, situations, and yourself. As you acknowledge your sacred connections to all, you'll note that you've been allowing your ego to dominate and contract your reasoning. Now you're ready to think expansively.

And you're also ready to communicate and interact with others in a more loving way, to respond to their egotistical behaviors with compassion instead of allowing your ego to battle theirs. Having accepted that we are all one, that caring for others fosters your own well-being, you're ready to create a better life for yourself and all of us.

These are the very practical lessons you'll learn in Part IV. They'll give you strength and courage no matter what you face, because you'll fully understand that you can embody Divine love regardless of what's happening around you.

•• ● ••

BRINGING WHOLELINESS INTO THE WORLD IN PRACTICAL WAYS

WHOLELINESS
AND EXPANSIVE
THINKING

*"I know nothing except
the fact of my ignorance."*

— SOCRATES

Thinking is much underrated! Those who say we have become imbalanced and devalued our intuitive abilities too much are correct. However, that doesn't mean we should overlook the power of the conscious, rational mind, for it is a powerful tool in helping us heal ourselves and our fellow human beings.

Our problem is not that we think too much, but that our thinking is flawed and contracted. Confining our minds is the great impediment of progress because it always carries with it a quality of fear—of the unknown, the unfamiliar, the future, and so on. This takes us away from the healing power of wholeliness and causes us to resist change. When our ideas are restricted, we see through a narrow lens and are essentially blind to all the other information available to us. We start to believe that if others don't see things our way, there's something wrong with them. Personal and group egos dominate our consciousness, and fear takes hold.

In contrast, expansive thinking involves a wide perspective and willingness to take in and synthesize the totality of what you see, hear, and come in contact with. It brings peace and power because it helps you recognize and cherish your sacred connections to: the past, present, and future; the invisible world; those who came before you; those yet to come; and all those whom you're sharing this planet with. It connects you to your creativity and keeps you flexible and resilient. Expansive thinking fosters optimism, and it helps you find opportunities within crises and tolerate the uncertainty you'll experience in times of transformation.

If you engage in intellectual exploration and creative, expansive thinking, you'll raise your consciousness, recognize that wholeliness connects us all, and feel closer to the Divine. As you expand your thinking, you'll become more spiritual, loving, and compassionate toward yourself and others. With healthy habits of the mind, you can achieve happiness and contentment even as you eagerly take up your responsibility to contribute to the healing of the world.

If you were fortunate enough to have a quality education, or to be exposed to many different ideas as a result of your life experiences, you're more likely to be an expansive thinker. But to develop expansive thinking doesn't demand high intelligence, extensive training, or special skills. It simply requires the courage to ponder information that makes you feel uncomfortable, listen carefully to new ideas and what others have to say, and take the time to consider new concepts.

In an era where there's enormous pressure to come up with instant opinions or quickly understand and make sense of a constant flood of information, it's easy to become insecure and uncomfortable with all that is expected of you. In this chapter, I'll show you how to let go of your ego's fear, reject the habit of contracted and limited thinking, and allow yourself to open your mind and expand your thinking. This will help you see connections that you couldn't detect before: to others who seem different from you; and between seemingly opposing ideas that will lead to better health, well-being, and more.

To expand your thinking, you'll have to ask a lot of questions, explore what others have done in similar circumstances, go back and take a second look at your past to learn from it, and acknowledge and address any biased thinking (including yours!). This will take effort and courage, as well as a blending of critical analysis and intuitive insights.

Let Go of Contracted Thinking: Nine Key Shifts You Must Make

At this point in our evolution as humans, *all* of us need to meet the challenge of expanding our thinking. You can begin to do so by making the following nine key shifts:

Shift #1: Be Aware of the Rules of Logic and Honor Them

People can disagree about facts, or give more weight to some than others, but the rules of logic always remain the same: two plus two will always equal four.

Now, we usually know the rules of logic, but sometimes our emotions get the better of us and we become irrational and illogical. We exaggerate or minimize facts we don't like, and justify our choices that defy common sense. Indeed, our feelings have a way of making us believe negative things that are just not true and engage in irrational thinking. The challenge is to calm our emotional turbulence and reexamine our thought processes.

It's only natural to lose sight of your standards when you're angry or anxious, but if you do, be sure to take the time later on to examine the disconnect in logic that got you to this point. This way, you can become aware of your biases and correct your thinking.

Shift #2:
Reject Pessimism and Embrace Optimism

Lower emotions such as fear, anger, and sadness commonly cause the bias of pessimism: seeing the present as fraught with problems and the future as holding only negative possibilities. When you fear the unfamiliar, you end up avoiding and resisting it. This also leads to resisting change.

When you lose something of importance, such as a romantic partner or a job, of course you feel upset or distraught, but then you may also allow your mind to start creating pessimistic thoughts. You insist that the future can't possibly bring you something that's as good as what you've lost.

I truly understand this mind-set. After I first arrived in America, I missed my family, home, and singing career, and I began to think of the U.S. as overrated and nowhere near as wonderful as my native country. To be honest, I was quite skeptical about my ability to find happiness living in America. At first, whenever my husband—who was also from Romania—pointed out a positive aspect of our adopted country, I countered this with a negative observation. Then I'd become nostalgic about home, overlooking all its problems (which were much larger than the problems in the U.S.).

Pretty soon, however, Virgil's optimistic attitude about all that this place could offer me helped shift me out of my negativity, and I decided to admit that he had a more balanced view. I began to look at America differently and release my pessimism . . . and thank goodness I did. I can't imagine where I'd be now if I hadn't taken in the totality of the adverse situation I had in Romania, compared with what I have here, and expanded my thinking.

When we project our melancholy and cynicism into the world, its response is to meet our expectations. For example, when I was unhappy and unsure about being in America, I inevitably saw the rude businessman pushing his way past me on the subway platform and overlooked the kind stranger who held the door for me. We all have to make the mind a sanctuary for positive thoughts, regularly ponder the more magical moments of life, and exercise the talents with which Spirit endowed us in order to create good karma. As we expand our thinking, we'll end up experiencing more joy in life because we will identify the potential good in all situations and people—including ourselves.

Shift #3:
Open Up to the Invisible World

You may have experienced what society deems a paranormal event, such as a precognitive dream or a visit from someone who has passed. If you didn't give in to fear and denial, you now know that there is an invisible world that is as real as it is mysterious. However, if you haven't experienced this other realm yet, here's what I've learned from being able to break linear time and access it: just one such experience can alter your perception and open your heart to wholeliness in a way that merely learning about such things does not.

It's crucial to simply believe in this place of expanded consciousness—and our sacred connections to it—so you can support yourself in your own healing and happiness. More important, though, is to actually experience this small miracle. I encourage you to have a reading with a qualified intuitive, and develop your own intuitive abilities. (In my book *Everyday Karma,* I offer many ideas for helping you awaken these skills we all share but which are often stifled by the conscious mind due to society's fear and disdain of them.)

Once you've had an encounter with the other side through a session with a medium or an accurate psychic prediction, you'll find yourself more open to the other "paranormal" ideas that are associated with wholeliness.

Shift #4:
Become Curious about—and Respect—
Others' Opinions and Perceptions

Contracted thinking involves giving too much weight to your individual experience, dismissing other people's opinions and perceptions in the process. Expansive thinking, on the other hand, means that you balance your beliefs with those of others. If someone's ideas don't mesh with yours, this doesn't mean that one of you is right and the other is wrong. You and this other person are simply looking at life from different angles, and neither of you can see the whole picture of human experience, which only the collective consciousness can truly comprehend. By embracing wholeliness and choosing to think broadly, you'll come closer to seeing the totality that escapes you when you're stuck in a limited point of view.

While personal reflections and interpretations are neither right nor wrong, we can be quite sensitive and defensive about them. We want to be seen and heard, and to have our theories validated and valued by others. We forget what a crucial role we play as individuals who are part of the larger whole, and we become too invested in being seen as right.

Wholeliness bestows confidence, which breeds patience and respect for others. In time, you'll find that you even enjoy being contradicted by other people when you're conversing, because you'll see that it stimulates you to be even more expansive in your thinking. You'll understand why the ancient Greeks and Romans revered the art of dialogue, seeing it as offering an opportunity for spiritual advancement. These were the true masters of philosophical debate—they believed that only through expressing individual opinions, questioning commonly held beliefs, and holding intellectual discussions could human beings attain higher truth.

Shift #5:
Accept That You Have Much to Learn

Our minds are often on autopilot, drawing upon the information we've acquired in our lives to understand our present situations. We think we're familiar with a person, a circumstance, or an event because it's similar to another one we've experienced in the past, but we're not seeing the total picture or opening ourselves to genuinely new perspectives and possibilities. To paraphrase Shakespeare, there are more things in heaven and earth than are dreamt of in our philosophies. There's much we all have to learn, but we can't do so if we contract our thinking.

Unfortunately, schools are more focused on preparing people to conform to society's expectations than on helping them develop broad-mindedness. And fears about financial insecurity have driven many young adults to study more technical subjects in college rather than the humanities or arts.

What's more, people's insecurities about intellectual shortcomings often lead them to avoid or even resent those who seem smarter or better informed. The increased disrespect for those who are educated—the classification of them as "inauthentic" or "elitist" —is rooted in this feeling of inadequacy that too many share. No one should be embarrassed by an inability to follow what his doctor is saying or an economist's complicated theory. An individual should not feel that she's betraying her social class if she earns a higher degree or reads books instead of watching television. A retreat into defensiveness results in a cessation of learning and exacerbation of shame.

Even the smartest, most educated people have holes in their knowledge and allow their bruised egos to affect their thinking. Consider your own insecurities: When faced with the possibility that your argument isn't sound or that you have something to learn, what happens to you? Do you tense up, become irritable, and not listen closely to the other person? If you find yourself reacting in this way to someone who has a more complete understanding of a topic, silently tell yourself, *This is a touchy subject for me. That's okay. I'm going to find the courage to expand my thinking.* In that moment, you can choose to feel compassion for yourself. Say the following prayer to the Divine for patience and self-love: *Please help me to heal my insecurity and trust that I can eliminate the biases in my thinking.*

As gratitude for this new perspective warms your heart, you'll now be able to look at these situations as prime opportunities for becoming wiser and more open-minded. You can also start to see yourself as a lifelong learner, looking to history, other cultures, and the arts to encourage expansive thinking and see connections you might otherwise miss.

Humanity is diverse; some people need to do more to develop their intellect, while others need to focus on showing more compassion for others. Harsh self-judgment is destructive. Wherever you are in your own learning process, be loving, gentle, and honest with yourself about what you still need to work on, and trust that you'll have help all along the way.

The best response to an uncomfortable intellectual challenge is to say to yourself, *Wait—maybe I can understand what this person is telling me if I invest a little more time and effort. Maybe I can connect it to something I already know.* Admitting that you have much to learn, and that there's plenty of information you have yet to encounter, will become easier over time as you banish your fear.

Shift #6:
Think Beyond Sound Bites
and Literal Interpretations

In our busy world, we often communicate in short, canned phrases that don't capture the complexity of our ideas or experiences. We need to slow down and take in the sweet richness of life, balancing these short exchanges with more detailed and nuanced dialogues that help us connect more intimately. We're doing a great disservice to our intellectual capacity when we only engage in petty chitchat that doesn't actually make us *think*.

Sound bites aren't just lacking in nuances; they actually hide the truth of a situation because they leave out important details. So don't get all your news from the headlines that crawl at the bottom of the TV screen, or consider yourself informed about world events if you only glance at the front page of the newspaper. That won't stimulate you intellectually or provide you with a broad or complete picture. Instead, involve yourself in deeper discussions. Read quality books and lengthy articles that challenge you intellectually. Get past the slogans on bumper stickers and protest signs to explore issues in depth.

Contracted thinking also causes us to take words too literally. Recall Plato's theory that I mentioned earlier, in which he stated that in the visible world we can only create inferior and limited versions of the infinite, perfect forms that exist in the other realm. A limited perception makes us believe that abundance is only to be found when we possess a lot of money or a particular body shape and facial features, for instance. Yet an expanded awareness allows us to come closer to those perfect forms of justice, beauty, love, abundance, wholeliness, and so on.

Expansive thinking lets us widen our ideas about these forms so that we can appreciate everything we have in our lives. Instead of feeling hurt and unfairly treated by the fates, we enjoy all of our blessings and recognize the support from Spirit.

Shift #7:
Take in and Digest Information Slowly

Increasingly, we're addicted to the technologies that bombard us with information—some of it extremely useful, some of it limited in value, and some of it just plain useless. It all comes at us so quickly that we feel we must take it in and digest it instantly. Just as we have to take the time to chew our food properly, we have to slow down and not let any old piece of information, regardless of its quality, come into our minds and become a part of our awareness. We're becoming distracted, even obsessed, by news that's meaningless or harmful because it triggers fear. I don't think we realize the negative effect that this is having on our brains.

We swim in a veritable sea of information every day. Because we have trouble prioritizing it and discerning what is of value, we tend to feel overwhelmed. Few of us have been trained to filter out the noise of the wired age or cut through the biases of those communicating their opinions. The best we can usually do is simply understand that many sources are quite slanted and try to dig through what we receive to unearth the facts. Then we're able to fill in our own understanding and check out other perspectives.

Rather than always getting your news from a source that's trying to compete with rivals to get the story first, regularly consult organizations that take the time to get the story *right*. Too often, we've seen news outlets quickly report on something that was actually false or whip up a frenzy of fear and worry about an incident that turned out to be unworthy of our attention. Slow down; be skeptical of what you see; and consider focusing more on reading stories of the week, month, or year than on the topic of the day or hour.

To help your "digestion" of all this information, participate in discussions that are free from negative emotions and don't trigger people's egos. There's little to be learned when individuals are calling each other names or dismissing their opponents as foolish or ignorant.

And discard the belief that you have to immediately understand complex ideas and then offer up an informed opinion. Anxiety about being seen as unintelligent will make you rush, and distort, your thinking process. If you don't know the latest controversial statement from a politician, that's perfectly okay. Overly saturating your mind with the heaps of information around you will neither add to your life nor subtract from it. That which isn't valuable, and doesn't contribute to the wisdom of the earth, isn't a component of wholeliness.

Slow down and take your time to develop your opinions and ideas, always remaining open to new and different perspectives. Being the first person in the room to come up with something isn't important. Developing wisdom and understanding from what you encounter is.

Shift #8:
Be Wary of Those Offering Wisdom for a Price

Many people are trying to feed us knowledge that is actually anything but, and it's just for their own egotistical reasons. They take advantage of us when they see how lost and desperate for wisdom we are. In the end, they disappoint us when the falseness in their teachings is inevitably exposed. The more powerful, rich, and famous they become, the more their egos take over and they expose their true motives.

If someone's advice revolves solely around how to make your life better as an individual and doesn't incorporate teachings about your responsibilities to the larger whole, it is false wisdom that's appealing to your ego.

All of us need to turn the focus on "me" into a focus on "we" *as well as* "me."

Shift #9:
Practice Appropriate Skepticism

A short while ago, a client called me for a session and immediately let me know that he didn't believe in mediumship or psychic abilities. I told him that I appreciated his honesty, and that a healthy amount of skepticism is always a good thing. I began to describe his wife who had died very recently (and correctly identified her unusual name), details of her death that only he and the doctors knew, and exactly what she looked like. He validated that I was correct and told me to keep going. I started to talk about his own past—which I often do in order to help people see patterns in their lives—when he cut me off, saying, "You could have learned all that about me on the Internet."

In response, I pointed out that much of what I'd told him wouldn't be available online since it was so obscure, and he grudgingly agreed. I also explained that if I could do that much research in the ten minutes between the time he called to set up the session and when we actually began, then I'd missed my calling, as I must be a research genius!

He confessed that what I was saying made sense, but then reaffirmed, "I don't know how you do it . . . but I don't believe in any of this."

Part of me was irritated, and part of me had to laugh at this perfect example of how we want to experience our sacred, healing connections—the wholeliness that binds us to those who have died, strangers, and the past and future—and yet our limited, contracted thinking holds us back.

Some people continue to cling to the notion that mediums and psychics are phonies who are somehow out to trick them. *Skeptic* comes from the Greek word *skeptikos,* which means "one who reflects upon," but today, those who call themselves skeptics don't openly examine what they don't understand so much as reject it. If someone hasn't experienced déjà vu, a precognitive dream, communication from the spirit world, or the ability to predict the future or instantly know something about a stranger's past, the appropriate skeptical response would be, "I don't know what that's about, so I'll withhold judgment for now as I explore it." To dismiss another person's opinion or encounter because we can't share it or get it to conform to the rules of a double-blind scientific study is to engage in limited, contracted thinking, and that's not genuine skepticism.

The world becomes smaller when we take on this attitude: *If I don't understand it—if I can't explain, predict, and control it— it doesn't have any value.* I'd like to see scientists become curious about paranormal activities, to study and learn more about them. Social scientists could look at these phenomena that are common to cultures all around the world and throughout history and ask, "How do such experiences affect someone else's perceptions and behaviors?" Small-mindedness holds individuals back from expansive thinking that would enrich all of our lives. Appropriate skepticism requires that we respect others' circumstances and beliefs, even if we don't share them or we interpret them differently.

People often play the role of the cynic or skeptic in order to appear powerful and important—and probably because they're feeling wounded and insecure. Be compassionate toward them and don't let them prick your own ego. Remain open and curious about the world and your experiences.

Creativity and Curiosity

All evolution is driven by the power of creativity, which flows naturally from a curious mind. Therefore, we should always question what's around us, the systems of life, and how we can improve them. We were born with an innate sense of inquisitiveness, but our innovative abilities are hampered by insular thinking; negativity; mental turmoil; unhealthy practices; and, unfortunately, the challenges of everyday life. How are we to think expansively when we feel constricted by our circumstances? How can we think outside the box when we feel as if we're *living* in a box?

The answer is to separate what we live from what we dream. We need to have curious minds and engage in wonder as we use logic and intuition together. We must look to the past and reclaim lost wisdom, while considering what's possible for the future.

Our modern world progressed to what it is today thanks to creative thinkers who allowed their grand ambitions to surpass the rest of society's modest goals. We need to aspire limitlessly as well, and then we must figure out how to act so that we can make our dreams a reality. We have to rediscover the power of creativity.

If the idea of being creative scares you because it doesn't seem very secure, know that creativity and stability are actually closely related. In fact, it's only when you're flexible, innovative, and bold that you can bring about the security you seek, for the ground will always be shifting under your feet. Resilience is your power.

Jesus said, "Unless you change and become like little children, you will never enter the kingdom of heaven" (Matthew 18:3). I'd like to adapt this slightly for our purposes and replace "enter the kingdom of heaven" with "experience wholeliness, peace, and power." We ought to aspire to be like children because they are both curious and creative. They haven't yet been exposed to the evils of the world or retreated into cynicism, pessimism, and contracted thinking. They haven't been conditioned to stubbornly cling to a certain notion, live a particular lifestyle, or adopt their parents' prejudices.

Kids naturally strive to expand their thinking every second of the day. For example, they ask question after question, open the box that their mothers told them not to, and come up with clever observations and insights that remind us of how contracted and uncreative our own thinking is! In this way, we should strive to be more like the curious little ones of the world.

Unfortunately, as adults who have witnessed injustice, suffered losses, and seen the worst of human nature, we've become jaded and cynical. The tragic events we've witnessed or endured have actually narrowed our mind-sets over time. We've forsaken the belief that humanity can redeem itself—yet now more than ever, we need to broaden our thinking and embrace hope, for that is the first phase of real change. The next step is expanding our thinking so that we can imagine our lives differently. We need to open to curiosity and wonder, tolerance and acceptance, and flexibility and the willingness to try something new. Then we can begin to shape the future.

How to Expand Your Thinking So That It Reflects Wholeliness

Observe

Observe your thinking patterns. How are they affected when you're fearful, anxious, or insecure? How does being angry change your thought processes? When are you most open, curious, creative, and optimistic? What helps you shift out of cynicism and into a sense of hopefulness? What awakens your sense of creativity and wonder?

As you contemplate your usual patterns of thought, identify the ways in which you're able to shift from constriction to expansion. When do you tend to make these shifts?

Use your journal to record the answers to these questions so that you're able to go back and reread what you've written.

Pray

Ask the Divine for clarity of mind: Pray to be freed of fear and ego-based defensiveness so that you can expand your knowledge and develop your analytical abilities. Pray that you may become more aware of your biases, and request the courage to let go of your prejudices, fear, grief, and anger. Pray that you might find ways to be more open-minded and imaginative in every area of your life. Pray to be shown ways in which you can challenge your mind to expand your viewpoints as you learn new concepts and theories.

Pray for our leaders, that they might broaden their thinking and become more creative. And when you observe someone with a limited perspective who's stirring up anger and fear, say a prayer that he or she might be healed of these lower emotions and start thinking more expansively.

Act

Engage in learning with great enthusiasm. Whatever you can think of doing to educate yourself, do it. Discover more about history, other cultures, and innovative ideas, and also keep up with the issues of today. Read up on all kinds of subjects, attend lectures, watch documentaries and educational films, study a new language, watch a foreign film, or read a novel originally published in another country. Contemplate how it is different from what you're used to.

Join a book club to help keep you motivated to read quality materials, or discussion groups where the topics challenge you and others to think creatively. Get together with those who have unique beliefs and experiences compared with your own, and truly listen to their ideas. Most important, make learning fun.

As you expand your thinking, it becomes easier to drop your ego's defensiveness, understand others, and find common ground. It also becomes easier to accept people as they are instead of trying to fix them. You recognize that healing the world doesn't mean forcing anyone else to think and perceive as you do, but rather to shift on the inside so that you aren't in battle mode and can positively influence those who are ready. You can assist others to awaken to wholeliness and let go of fear when you're not striving to "fix" anyone.

In time, great shifts in human awareness will occur. Small-mindedness, bigotry, and hatred will become increasingly rare. As you participate in this evolution of consciousness and the human experience, you must be very patient and loving.

Next, you'll discover the best ways to interact with those who will challenge you to potentially trigger your fearful and defensive ego, drawing you away from wholeliness. Although it can be very tempting to try to control or change others, this must be resisted if you're to experience wholeliness and participate in the healing of all—which begins by embodying love.

•• ● ••

WHOLELINESS
AND RELATIONSHIPS
WITH OTHERS

*"We are on this earth with work to do,
and relationships are like laboratories
where the work gets done."*

— MARIANNE WILLIAMSON

Abstractly, it's easy to love others. But how do we love those who seem unlovable? Jesus said "Love your enemies" (Matthew 5:44), but how exactly do we do that?

All human beings strive for unconditional love, and all religions embrace the concept. Unfortunately, we tend to fall short of this ideal. When we can't comprehend how we could possibly love those who don't show the same affection, respect, and kindness to us in return, we begin to become quite cynical. How can we thrive if we love those who are selfish or cruel?

Because of our negative emotions and contracted thinking, we often limit our love, sometimes subconsciously and unintentionally. As clients I've counseled have told me, "I can't forgive that person. He's horrible and he hurt me too badly. Who am I, Jesus Christ?" The gap between total forgiveness and what we feel capable of is very wide. But when we embrace wholeliness, we recognize that we *can* love unconditionally. We can forgive and allow karma to create the natural consequences that will heal both the transgressor and ourselves.

If you've never experienced what it's like to feel love for someone when he's acting unlovable, open your heart to wholeliness . . . and soon you'll know the deep sense of peace and power that comes from doing so. You'll transcend your weaknesses and feel your sacred connection to the Divine and all the love in the world. Your ego will recede as you wonder in joy and amazement, *Where did this incredible ability to love come from?* And in an instant, you'll know that it's from a sacred source beyond the world of the senses. Only Spirit can endow you with such a pure emotion.

As you look into the eyes of someone who is raging in anger or heaping contempt upon you, unconditional love allows you to realize that this person can't hurt your spirit or trigger your ego's response. You'll realize that you're not alone, and that you're walking with angels and being filled with the Divine in that moment.

Every single human being has the capacity to feel this way. As you embrace wholeliness, you'll come to know this remarkable experience, and your faith in the healing power of your sacred connections will grow in a way that you never imagined. It's as if God's love has turned you into a beacon of light and freed you from the burdens of fear, anger, and sadness. This love awakens the higher mind of reason, perceives the pain in others, and allows you to give with no expectation of receiving anything in return—all the while showing you the perspective to maintain strong boundaries with those incapable of accepting what you're offering.

You can learn to love unconditionally, rise above your ego's desire to change others, and accept them just as they are right now. There's comfort in knowing that such positive, pure emotion opens people's hearts to the transformative power of wholeliness.

Be aware that your influence may not be immediate, or that your love may touch the heart of someone else you're not even aware of, but the effect is always real and very powerful. You can transform yourself *and* participate in the evolution of all humanity.

Then cynicism and fear will move on to find a new home, and love will illuminate your path and accompany you with each step.

The Six Challenges to Wholeliness

In this chapter, I'll describe six challenges that you'll encounter as you strive toward wholeliness. Although I've covered loving unconditionally up to this point, it is just one of these objectives you'll be required to master. What follows is a list of all six:

- Let go of the need to fix or rescue others

- Love unconditionally and give with no expectation of a reward

- Communicate with love

- Listen with an open mind and open heart

- Risk being honest with yourself and others

- Be patient with yourself and others

As you undertake these challenges, always remember that all interactions, even brief conversations with strangers, offer you a chance for internal transformation and to change the larger whole through shifting your energy and behaving differently. Every day will present you with opportunities to achieve these goals. Stay awake to them, and do what you know you must, because then you'll begin to experience your sacred connections. Pass the Divine's test for you: show compassion in all circumstances.

Here's a look at the six challenges in detail:

Challenge #1:
Let Go of the Need to Fix or Rescue Others

When you see a problem, it's only natural to want to rush in and fix it. Yet the naïve belief that you can rescue another person very often results in that individual feeling hurt or resentful. You can certainly offer others your assistance, but you have to accept that they have free will and are ultimately going to make their own decisions.

Remember that the ego sees through a lens of individuality, perceiving everyone as a separate, detached being. Thus, your ego believes that you only have the ability to directly influence a specific person—which means that it has great difficulty accepting the reality of the invisible world, where the butterfly effect takes place.

If your ego can't see the immediate, tangible results of your actions, it assumes that your energy disappeared into the ether and that your efforts were in vain. It doesn't realize that simply by creating good karma, you're having an effect on yourself, which in turn means that you're influencing the whole. So in your relationships with others, don't let your ego direct your decisions. Trust in the power of the good karma you create.

There may also be silent witnesses who are inspired by your loving actions to generate good karma themselves. A friend of yours might tell the story of your strength and courage, and the listener, totally inspired, may retell it—which then inspires someone else to find her courage and act from a place of unconditional love. And you may never even know of this chain of reactions. The ego, unaware of the way the invisible world works, refuses to believe in the miraculous, rippling effects of creating good karma.

You have information and skills that you can share with others for their benefit because, having a good and loving heart, you naturally want to help. At times, you'll have better insights into people's issues than they do, and may feel compelled to share your wisdom. But don't let your ego become too domineering and convince you that you can offer unwanted advice or take on someone else's problem as your own. The ego will blind you to possibilities you might not have considered—including the fact that you could be wrong and actually don't know what's best for that person! Maybe what he needs isn't advice, but simply loving acceptance that will give him the courage to change his actions.

No one wants to see those they care about suffer, but suffering is a part of life. When you truly accept this, you shift your ego's desire to fix others, repair the political system, or save the world.

You recognize that you can participate in the *process* of helping others help themselves. Trust that your loving actions will have a powerful effect on the whole, and that suffering won't be in vain.

When you try to rescue another person from a painful situation or the consequences of her actions, you prevent her from resolving her own karma. She needs to work through her pain and bring about growth from within. There really is only so much you can do before you must step back. Instead, just offer assistance and support. Allow her to express free will by accepting that each person is on an individual path that is part of the larger human journey.

The peace and power you experience when you embrace wholeliness will allow you to balance your desire to contribute to the well-being of others with your longing to trust in the perfection of creation. Marvel at the mystery of how good karma affects the whole, and you'll find that your anxious desire to improve others will subside and be replaced by the healthy aspiration to help where you can. Accept that sometimes you can't resolve a problem, because it's not yours to resolve.

Keep in mind that after an unsuccessful attempt by Jesus and his disciples to bring wisdom to a certain town, he told the disciples to shake the dust off their shoes and move on to the next one. We all need to recognize when it's time to shake the dust off our own shoes and focus our energy on more positive pursuits than trying to force others to rise into higher awareness.

Challenge #2:
Love Unconditionally and Give
with No Expectation of a Reward

When you offer unconditional love, you have no expectation of receiving anything in return from that person. When you give from a place of pure love, the joy you feel within yourself makes it all worthwhile.

It's very difficult to love unconditionally, however, because the insecure ego is afraid of giving to others without the guarantee of receiving a tangible reward in kind—be it appreciation and thanks, public recognition, or something else. The ego doesn't trust that the universe will always provide. If you lovingly give to others, the feelings of lack and fear (such as that you won't have enough money, time, or energy to take care of yourself) will start to fade.

Even if your giving takes a lot of time, patience, or emotional strength, you'll find yourself energized rather than depressed *if* you're coming from a place of unconditional love. Because you're receiving Divine love, your soul is being nourished and rejuvenated, and generosity allows this gift from Spirit to filter through your soul. When you absolutely must stop and replenish yourself with a meal, good night's sleep, or a few hours of silence, you'll be able to listen to your inner voice and attend to the needs of your body, mind, and spirit. You can do this because you aren't giving out of a desperate and fearful need to prove what a good parent, child, employee, or spouse you are. You're giving for the sake of yourself and others.

• • •

Our communities are crying out for help, and plenty of people are sympathetic to their neighbors' distress but feel guilty because they don't pitch in. They think they simply don't have the time or energy to help. Feeling compassion, they'll give money to charities, sign petitions, or write to their representatives, which are noble and important acts. But to actually experience the act of giving to others from a pure heart provides joy and the uplifting energy to keep on giving.

The potential for acting generously is all around you. In fact, if you do an Internet search for "volunteer opportunities" in your town or city, you might be surprised at all the possibilities that are posted. If you're the type of person who prefers to do tasks that don't involve meeting new people because you're timid, then start with volunteering for an assignment that doesn't involve much social interaction. But don't be surprised if you find yourself so excited by being able to serve that one day you offer to let someone else work in the back office while you greet strangers or lead tours. You'll make new friends who share your interests and feel a sense of purpose, all because you let go of your fears and gave from the heart.

Unconditional love and giving is important closer to home, too. Gently offer a different, more hopeful perspective to the people in your life who are depressed, angry, or despairing. If someone is anxious and worried, share evidence of the power of hope with him, and let him know that you will support him 100 percent as he works to improve his situation. Encourage individuals who are feeling pessimistic to watch uplifting movies or videos, read empowering books, and join you in volunteering in the community. Point out that their cynicism seems to be draining them: "You seem so upset about that situation. I wonder, is there anything you can do to help alleviate the problem? Maybe together we can do something." Such encouragement will help others start feeling a sense of wholeliness.

Whenever you can, offer the gift of your time. People who feel lonely and disconnected often think that no one cares about them. Instead of plopping down on the couch to watch TV for a few hours every night after work, why not pick up the phone and call someone you know who struggles with loneliness? Or, better yet, get together with her in person. The gift of time is a precious commodity nowadays. If you can take even an hour here or there to devote to one who needs support, you'll be performing an act of great kindness. There's nothing more uplifting to someone who struggles than to see a friend walk through her door ready to listen.

When you support someone through listening, it's important to hear her complaints, but offer a way to see through a more positive lens as well. A good question to ask is: "Tell me one good thing that happened today," and encourage her to relish that event, even if it was a seemingly small moment in a very stressful day. If you're filled with Divine love and feeling your sacred connections, you'll find it easier to pay attention to what she has to say without becoming angry or depressed yourself. The acceptance and encouragement you freely give can be a healing balm that helps your friend shift into a more optimistic frame of mind.

What's more, assisting others will cause your own feelings of being lonely, unappreciated, and unimportant to fade. You'll be assured that just as you give to others, there are those who are ready to do the same for you. You'll also start to see that doing good is as energizing as taking a brisk walk, while at the same time it will make you sleep more soundly and peacefully at night.

Challenge #3:
Communicate with Love

In all relationships and interactions, always communicate with love. If you care about a person, you'd most likely agonize over how to deliver bad news to him in the least upsetting way. But if someone hurts you, you may not make such a loving choice. Your feelings of shame, sadness, or animosity could be paralyzing —the fearful ego, perceiving that it's under threat, may urge you to lash out in self-protection.

Before you react, it's always best to look at the totality of the individual who is causing you pain. His behavior may be due to his own insecurities, which probably have very little to do with you. Yet he may be taking his anger out on you simply because he desperately needs to let out his emotions.

Find the power to strengthen the love between you and this fellow human being. Visualize a white light surrounding both of you, and then ask yourself: *Why can't this person be patient and respectful toward me right now? Could there be something going on inside of him that I might help heal?*

As I've said before, it's not your responsibility to solve others' problems for them, but if you release your ego's fear and feel compassion for them, you empower yourself. People are utterly surprised if, in the midst of their screaming fit, you respond with a soothing voice and an understanding approach. This sort of reaction then calms their ego, often in an instant.

Wholeliness will give you the equanimity to speak just the right words. Instead of robotically retaliating against a statement, say something like, "I completely understand why you would say that, but here's what I think . . . ," and then state your opinion. Or try, "I'm not sure I understand . . . ," and ask a question that will help you grasp what this person is saying.

To say, "You seem to be in quite a hurry," and then patiently step back may well trigger someone to push ahead of others and get to the front of a line. Even if she doesn't respond with an apology and a willingness to wait her turn, you've at least made it possible that she'll leave the situation thinking about how gently and kindly you pointed out her unfair behavior. Remember, unconditional love doesn't always produce immediate, observable results.

• • •

There are many ways to draw someone's attention to his destructive behavior and creation of bad karma without having a confrontation. Personally, I'm not in favor of the word *confront,* because it almost always denotes an argument to follow. Simply ask, "Do you feel that this approach to the problem is working for you?" "You seem unhappy with this situation. Is that what I'm picking up on?" or "Are you thinking about trying to change the situation? What ideas have you explored?"

If he quickly becomes defensive, it's likely that he knows his behavior isn't working for him, but he's afraid to change or doesn't know how to do so. In this case, what he most needs is encouragement to believe that he can transform his actions, thoughts, and emotions, and that he'll have support along the way. Lovingly offer to help in any way you can, but don't scold him or tell him what he needs to do. Once people are told what to do, they instinctively want to do just the opposite. The ego doesn't like having someone else come up with the solution to its problem!

If the person says something that shocks or offends you, try not to become angry. It may simply be the ego lashing out, and you'd do well to avoid such battles. If you're having trouble remaining cool, stop the conversation and leave. Come back when you can communicate with love, even if that means you have to take a few minutes to pray or meditate before resuming. On occasion, you may need to let a few days or even weeks pass before you can continue the dialogue. Temporarily putting distance and time between you and the individual you aren't seeing eye to eye with isn't a negative approach. Everyone's ego calms down at different rates—after a heated argument, it can take people a substantial amount of time before their compassion kicks in and they can admit that they might have reacted irrationally or too harshly.

If you're anticipating a conflict with someone, say a prayer for patience and compassion before you begin speaking with her. Ask the Divine to help you find the right words and remain calm, loving, and strong. Imagine that the conversation will be positive and productive, and commit to doing your part to make it so.

Note that every conflict offers a chance to create an experience of cooperation in which you and another person can further expand your thinking and experience wholeliness. If you remain polite, and keep your words and tone of voice respectful, you'll invite the individual to explore her own karmic issues that are making her short-tempered or irritable. You'll also help her begin to wonder why she's not communicating effectively. Perhaps she'll learn a valuable lesson about how to better express her ideas. Acknowledge the totality of the person, and invite her to step out of defensiveness, fear, and anger and into compassion and cooperation.

Challenge #4:
Listen with an Open Mind and Heart

It's difficult to listen to ideas when they contradict yours. But if you find yourself actually becoming angry with someone who is simply explaining his personal viewpoints, then you've become entirely too attached to your opinions. Your task is to expand your outlook and embrace wholeness, so temporarily suspend your fondness for your beliefs. Just because this other individual has an opposing perspective doesn't mean that he's wrong and you have to fix him.

As much as an agreement between two people is fantastic, there's a certain beauty in the diversity of beliefs. See the value in this person's statements, and look beyond what he's saying to what he's feeling. Does he have a life experience that's very different from yours? If so, what can you learn from him? How can you expand your thinking about him? How can you use this conversation to express unconditional love for you both?

Examine your reaction honestly. Are you getting defensive because this person's reasoning is actually intriguing you or making you aware that you're not entirely comfortable with your own position? Could it be that your ego, and not your higher self, is responding?

Never be afraid to engage in a conversation with someone who thinks very differently from you or has a way of life you find hard to understand or accept. It's your ego that instills in you fear of "the other" and convinces you that you're under attack when you're just talking! If you feel intimidated by an entire group of people, approach just one of them and politely voice your concerns, but also look for what you have in common with this individual. As I said before, the mutual exchange of ideas—that is, taking turns asking questions and providing answers—and drawing fair conclusions is the path toward the highest truth and manifesting wholeliness.

Holding wholeliness as an ideal in your heart will make it easier to perceive the commonalities between you and others. Don't get caught spending too much time thinking about how you want to solve the problems of the world when you could be taking action to better understand those who seem different from you. Take the initiative, break out of your comfort zone, and reach out to embrace them.

Challenge #5:
Risk Being Honest with Yourself and Others

Being honest allows you to set healthy boundaries with others that help keep you safe. So if people tend to be abusive toward you, speak up—they may not have the self-awareness to recognize just how disrespectful their behavior is. If they don't have the ability to change, or if they're not capable of caring about or respecting you, then they need to work on themselves. People need time to understand what they've done wrong, and there's a loving but solid way to let them know how you feel.

When you're ready to begin to communicate with someone again, whether it's a family member you haven't spoken to in years or a former friend who has contacted you in the hope of rekindling your once-close connection, listen to your heart. Are you open to trusting that this person has changed? Or do you have to heal some of your own wounds first?

As apologetic as an individual can be, he may not be as ready to start anew as he thinks he is; after all, people can overestimate how much they've changed. Stressful situations can also trigger old behaviors, so proceed cautiously. Love that person, but be ready to put the relationship on hold again at the first sign that he isn't truly ready to treat you well. If you love him *and yourself* unconditionally, your most thoughtful choice might be to keep a firm boundary in place and not attempt to rekindle what you once had. Remember, you need to place your health and safety as the first priority, and you may not be ready to risk being hurt again. There's no shame in admitting that.

Whether or not you and this individual ever make peace in this lifetime, you'll be able to let go of your pain, anger, and resentment after you leave behind your bodies and return to the invisible world. You may end up meeting again in another life to work through your issues, or perhaps you'll work out your wounds with other people separately. However your karma plays out, you don't have to compromise and let someone treat you abusively for the sake of maintaining a relationship now. Be honest about how much you both really have changed.

While it might be necessary to work on the karmic issues that draw you to a specific friend, partner, or family member, you don't necessarily have to work on them with that particular person. Continue on your path of healing, but be honest with yourself about whether you can handle a relationship emotionally. As much as it's important to try to resolve your karma with everyone in your life, it's also okay to let go of someone.

Challenge #6:
Be Patient with Yourself and Others

It's easy to observe all of the flaws that the human race exhibits. When ugly behavior and cruelty surround us, it can be very difficult to have faith in our capacity to evolve and transform. People can change dramatically, but that doesn't mean *you* can change them one bit! All you can do is be honest and loving in your interactions with them, and exercise patience as they work through what they need to in their own way and in their own time.

We expect individuals to listen to our advice or insights and then instantly respond with gratitude and understanding, which is unrealistic. Emotional and mental shifts don't happen immediately —good karma affects people *in due time.* In fact, it may take someone years to come around to accepting the truth about his situation.

Speak to people with honesty and love, and then let go of your need to make them process what you're saying and have an instant turnaround. *If it's meant to happen, it will, but only after the person truly acknowledges what he must do to change.*

I used to have a client who was also a good friend. During one of my sessions for her, I saw that her boyfriend of seven years was cheating on her, and felt I had to tell her the truth. It was very difficult, but I truly believed that it was the best thing to do. My friend became so upset with me that she refused to speak to me for almost three years; she swore that I was lying, trying to ruin the relationship, and completely wrong to tell her this.

However, she ultimately discovered that what I'd told her was indeed true. It took her some time to reflect after that shock, but she eventually did come around. One day she decided to call me, and in the course of our conversation, she explained what had happened back then. She said that she should have known that I had only good intentions in telling her what I'd seen, and asked for my forgiveness. Of course I forgave her, but I also reassured her that I would never lie to her or try to hurt her. After this experience, we became closer than ever, and now trust each other implicitly.

It's difficult to be patient with others, especially when they pull away from us for having been honest with them, but people need time to accept painful truths. If someone's behavior is actually harming you or another, you must still be patient and loving. Don't blatantly accuse this person or tell him that he's wrong, as being forceful and aggressive will not cause him to move more quickly toward healing his karma. Instead, it will shut him down and cause him to withdraw into an ego response of defensiveness and denial.

In the midst of your own suffering and discomfort, be patient with yourself. You may not realize how much you're evolving as a result of choosing good karma over bad. It's easy to obsess about your problems, as well as about how challenging it is to transform your thought processes and behavior. Don't let your ego's impatience influence you. If you made the mistake of getting into a bitter argument because of your pride, forgive yourself and trust that you'll act more wisely next time. Your soul knows that change takes tolerance and restraint, and that you are blossoming right on schedule.

Whenever you're feeling tired or worn-out, finding it difficult to act lovingly, pray for patience. Ask Spirit and all those who are watching over you to help you love yourself more deeply and sense the strength of your sacred connections. Even as you pray and meditate, you'll start to notice your frustration lift as your heart fills with love and courage. You'll begin to have faith in yourself and your ability to navigate the sometimes-choppy waters of relationships. Your ego will become calm, your burdens lightened by the realization that the Divine is supporting you. Soon it will be easier to laugh, let go, and love more deeply. Know that your sacred connections bind you to love at all times and will give you the power to transform the quality of your life.

How to Bring Wholeliness
into Your Relationships with Others

Observe

When someone's unwilling to listen to you and you feel frustrated, ask yourself: *Why is it so important to me that I convince this person to see things my way? Is it my ego insisting that I dominate this situation? Is my attitude one of love and compassion? Am I balanced enough to be able to accept someone as he or she is right now?*

Take some time to identify which activities help you feel your sacred connections to other people. Think about how you might engage in them more regularly. And observe how individuals in your community are helping each other. Over the course of one day, write down all the evidence you'll find of people looking out for each other. Ponder how you might do more to help your fellow man.

Be sure to take the time to write out any reflections you have from these observations in your journal.

Pray

Pray for all those who brought food to your table. Say grace over a meal, expressing gratitude for your sacred connections and the many people who support you—from the farmer to the grocer, from your family members and friends to the co-worker who encourages you to believe in yourself.

Ask for peace to be brought to those who would harm you or are unable to treat you well. Pray that they may be healed and that you may overcome your own fear of being hurt. Pray that you and those you're in conflict with awaken to the humanity you share, come from a place of conditional love, and find common ground. Ask for the strength to act from your highest, most loving self and to love unconditionally.

Request that Spirit present you with opportunities to act in loving ways that will uplift and heal others, helping them feel their sacred connections. The Divine will always answer this prayer. By asking to have your eyes opened, you ensure that you will see the world differently.

Act

Replace a portion of the time that you spend on yourself with doing something to assist others. There are infinite possibilities in which you can create good karma and reawaken yourself and others to the healing that we all require.

Also, work on your communication skills. Make a difficult phone call or bring up a painful subject with someone you haven't been completely honest with in the past. Speak with love, patience, and acceptance; and trust that the outcome will be exactly what it is meant to be. Whatever happens, thank Spirit for the opportunity to deepen your connections to this person and ask that you both be filled with unconditional love for yourselves and each other.

Know that you and every other person are connected in wholeliness. You are brother and sister, mother and father, child, friend, and cousin to all who ever lived or shall walk this earth. Strife is an illusion of the ego that you can give energy to or heal with the love that flows to you from the Divine Force that gives life to each seed, every creature, and all dreams of a better world. Never forget your sacred connections.

AFTERWORD

Where Are We Going?

If we were to take humanity's current temperature, we'd find that most everyone is increasingly uncertain and worried about tomorrow—and rightfully so, because the systems that we've so faithfully established are losing stability and becoming less functional than ever. We're starting to understand that things are coming to an end, yet in many more ways, we feel as if we're on the brink of a new beginning. Inside of ourselves, we detect tremendous change and upheaval, just as an animal senses an approaching storm.

Since the dawn of humanity, our world has been run by just a handful of people, almost a secret society, who have commanded the destinies of all. Indeed, we've been controlled in one way or another by the whims and wills of our leaders and political figures. But this will not hold true in the future. The prophecies of the ancients, such as the Apocalypse and the end of the Mayan calendar, are about to be fulfilled, but not necessarily with the wildly devastating results we've imagined. Without a doubt, the planet *is* in the middle of a crisis that it has never before experienced. Everything seems to be crumbling . . . and I mean that literally, from the statues of politicians and powerful individuals coming down to structures literally collapsing due to a spike in natural disasters.

Our saving grace lies in acknowledging the totality of what is happening. We must admit that these developments are affecting us all in the same manner. In these dramatic situations, during which nobody seems to understand anything, people are desperately searching for answers to the "big questions": Where is God? Who are we? Why is this happening? Is there life on other planets? In seeking a profound change, we've begun to research the larger scope of our existence. We're starting to realize that this predicament will amplify if the human race doesn't become involved in transcending it.

Consider that there are almost seven billion souls on Earth, yet there's an extreme lack of ecological balance. The greater the number of people living here, the more the world becomes depleted of natural resources, various species of animals die out because of our intervention, and we cause dangerous climate change. Think of this irony: We, whom Mother Earth has given birth to, are meant to maintain harmony and ensure her health—yet we're doing just the opposite. We're bringing harm to the planet and each other.

Reasons for Hope

Despite our negative tendencies, the human spirit yearns to raise the consciousness of our species now more than ever. We long to enforce equal rights; learn from this wave of Internet information; and free our souls from binding, earthly restrictions.

And, in fact, the dark era *is* coming to an end. Many people have begun to fathom that this is the beginning of the golden era that we've been heralding for thousands of years. The human race has finally matured, exactly like teenagers going through the necessary and turbulent years of confusion and unrest while they're trying to grasp who they are. We've reached our peak of growth, and now we're finally moving up the scale of evolution that's equipped with a superior level of experience and incredible complexity. The real world, as it exists now, will soon become just a distant memory of the epoch of darkness. The very moment humanity comes to understand the truth about wholeliness—and collectively joins forces—life on Earth will change completely. We stand on the edge of an incredible planetary transformation, during which we'll acknowledge the reality of who we are and emerge into the light of knowledge.

Be prepared to let go of everything you think you've known in order to live a new life. Be ready for the most extraordinary adventure to rediscover truth, beyond what the human mind could have imagined. Leave behind your misconceptions, open your heart and mind, and reprogram all of your concepts in order to create a new future. More than anything else, think about the unifying message of this book, which is essential to a better way of life.

Together we are finally succeeding in unraveling the mysteries of the universe and the laws of matter. From Newtonian physics to the theories of Albert Einstein, from the discoveries of quantum physics to the phenomenon of nonlocality, humanity has reached the conclusion that in the universe exists quantum energy that influences each of us. Since we're all made of this energy, we're all impacted by the same forces.

The key to our power is to acknowledge that we are all one *and* part of the Divine at the same time. If we believe this statement, we can achieve things we never thought would be possible, and we'll be granted powers we never dreamed of. There's a unique energy that flows through us, and it's called love. To shun it is to deny our true existence.

December 21, 2012

In the last six billion years or so, every planet and satellite in our system has made a certain number of rotations, all to reach a *perfect alignment.* And this alignment will happen on December 21, 2012. This is the phenomenon that the Mayans so precisely calculated. It is also the reason we've seen more and more energy in our solar system, which has caused the planets to appear brighter, lighter, and warmer. In addition to affecting our solar system, this energy, because it's so alive and intelligent, has entered our bodies. It activates our DNA and enlightens our minds, thereby spurring us to take a step forward. Yet it escalates tensions on a large scale in the political, economic, religious, and social worlds as well.

Our perception is expanding, and we are beginning to comprehend that time is more than a three-dimensional idea now that we have an awareness of the parallel reality that exists beyond our universe. Thus, there is another element of time. Einstein established the notion of the space-time continuum, but we'll soon discover that we can actually move through the three dimensions of time: the astral space, the dream space, and the paranormal space.

Our own planet is also raising its vibration, and this will be a liberation. In its movement through the galaxy, Earth is entering a great field of vibration that will change human DNA, allowing us to have incredibly long life spans. During this time, we will finally understand the necessity of honoring life and the Divine. The moment humanity reaches unity with Spirit will be the moment we witness true reality. The world around us will take on new meaning and new importance. We're entering a golden age in which the cosmic cycle of darkness is definitively ending because we're making contact with Spirit.

Because humanity *will* embrace wholeliness, the following predictions are based on how this will influence life on earth:

— December 21, 2012, will not be a doomsday or the end of the world—but we *are* headed toward great suffering and climate changes if we don't break out of our denial and begin to raise our consciousness. We must change the course of human history. The date of the winter solstice in the year 2012, the end of the Mayan calendar, has the energy of 11 (1 + 2 + 2 + 1 + 2 + 0 + 1 + 2 = 11), which, according to numerology, is the number of enlightenment. This is the official beginning of a new era in the human experience, of raised consciousness, as we evolve into beings with greater awareness and understanding of our Divine nature.

In connection with this, the satellites surrounding the earth will be affected during 2012, indirectly speeding up the process of change in financial institutions. Because the satellites will become temporarily unavailable, people will scramble to create alternatives to the systems that have been automatically regulated by those satellites.

As we approach the end of the Mayan calendar, things will become more challenging. Both 2011 and 2012 are years of awakening, as we start to realize how serious our situation is. Just as 2010 was the year of physical earthquakes, 2011 will be the year of "political earthquakes." We'll start to witness what happened in Egypt all around the world. People will take to the streets in rebellion against their dishonest leaders and jaded systems. More and more often, dictators and tyrants will be dethroned by those who they've ruled over.

Eventually, world leaders will begin to come together to imagine new economic systems and ways of dealing with climate change and natural disasters. Even further in the future, the world will have but one form of leadership governing every part of the globe.

— In the years to come, the numerous monetary systems all over the world will be condensed into one. We'll find new ways to be reimbursed for our labor, pay for goods, and so on. We will come to the realization that paper money needs to be replaced with a more efficient alternative—thus, we will develop electronic currency. In addition, the countless banks that exist today will converge into one single bank that spans the globe. As always, one system must die out to give birth to an improved one.

— We'll finally see that our economy and financial markets are not improving because the issues are much deeper than we can imagine. The European economy will deteriorate first, aggravating the global economy. The rate of unemployment will increase, and, interestingly, many people will begin to work from their homes via the Internet.

Acting as separate nations, we cannot hope to fix the problem. Almost every place in the world is experiencing financial collapse, meaning that we're all in this together. Therefore, we must rectify the economy together. We've been looking at the matter ethnocentrically, but our approach needs to shift to a global one. Only by developing one international financial system will the economy become whole and healed. Money will no longer be the root of all evil.

— The world may go through a state of chaos, which is necessary for progress, but this won't last for very long. In particular, we will witness intense, natural commotions in our universe: There will be increased cosmic radiation, more earthquakes and volcanic eruptions scattered around the globe, and a spike in solar activity. The activity of Schumann resonances (electromagnetic waves in the atmosphere) will peak, making it seem as if physical time is moving faster than it really is. More and more floods will inundate various parts of the planet, and Earth's rotation will slow down. The global temperature will fluctuate and be hard to anticipate, resulting in a decrease in the population of sea creatures and fauna.

Even if we also see institutions collapsing and our leaders in trouble, be assured that these are only temporary instances of disorder brought on for the advancement of the human race.

— I believe that human DNA will increase in complexity, thereby expanding our mental capacity and the level of our perception. We will begin to understand that we're all connected to the Divine Force in the same way. We'll acknowledge that all forms of life are actually a part of Spirit, under whom we are united as one. We'll finally realize that the different religions and gods of the world that we've held on to throughout centuries have been far too effective in helping us create hatred, war, anger, and separation.

Further, the Catholic Church will continue to experience problems, especially in regards to pedophilia and its wrongful hostility toward homosexuals. Pope Benedict XVI will be the last Pope before we see a universal unity of religions. A widespread change in the belief system of humankind is upon us—in fact, we are already starting to come together under a common belief system, and more and more people will regard death as simply a transition from the human body into a higher dimension of being. As we shift from religion to spirituality, individuals will use their abilities to harness energy for the purposes of healing, to interact with others, and to create positive changes.

— Humanity will come together in terms of leadership. The long-ruling systems of monarchy, papacy, presidency, dictatorship, and so on won't survive. For example, Queen Elizabeth II will be replaced by Prince William, and he will be the last king of the British monarchy. We'll see more people of faith guiding the world toward coming together as one global family. As a result, we'll accept each other the way we are, help out in ways we never have before, and love each other unconditionally. This might sound quite utopian, but the golden era that's approaching will create a paradise, the way the earth was originally designed.

— The global population will reach seven billion before the date of December 21, 2012. It is interesting to note that, according to United Nations estimates, the population entered the six billion mark around October 12, 1999. Now, almost exactly 12 years later, we have increased to one billion more. In terms of numerology, the number 12 represents a perfect cycle of time, so it seems that we are in accordance with the Divine calculations of the universe. The fact that the number of people in the world is reaching seven billion also foretells that we will reclaim our connection to the Divine: seven is a sacred number, the number of God, and we will soon become seven billion souls united by our mutual faith in one all-powerful Spirit.

Ironically, we had to wait until this time in history to reach this level because humanity is only now entering the golden era and able to raise its consciousness. Before this time, we were killing each other and not knowing why—it was because we were not *allowed* to hit this significant number seven as a population and evolve. Only now are we equipped with enough wisdom, love, and desire for unity to exist under the influence of such a Divine number. I predict that once we collectively reach the seven billion mark, we will stop killing each other.

— Brilliant new discoveries in the medical field will be aimed at reversing the aging process, and human beings will live much longer. As a result, we'll enjoy healthier, more fulfilling, more peaceful lives in harmony with nature and each other. We'll no longer depend on so many drugs, and we won't suffer physically or experience so much fear.

Our life spans will increase due to several different factors. Probably the most significant is that our DNA is transforming. Carbon 12, the very basis of the human body, will transmute into carbon 7. Carbon 12 currently is composed of 6 protons, 6 neutrons, and 6 electrons, lending it the energy of 6-6-6 . . . which the book of Revelation in the Bible renders as the "number of the beast." Until now, due to carbon 12's frequency in the natural world, we have been greatly influenced by this energy, which has manifested itself throughout human history in war, hatred, killing, and a tendency toward destruction.

Very soon, however, the components of carbon within our DNA will change into 6 protons, 1 neutron, and 6 electrons: 6-1-6, the components of carbon 7. Just as carbon 12 influenced our DNA negatively, carbon 7 will affect us in a positive manner. This change in our genetic makeup will amplify multidimensional thought and lead to higher levels of understanding. Thus, we will begin to see death as a transition to a new plane of existence, and once and for all decipher the mystery of life after death.

History has referred to this interesting element in symbolic ways. The concept of Metatron's Cube contains 13 equal circles: six circles are placed in a hexagonal pattern around one central circle, while the other six extend out along the same radial lines. Further, in Leonardo da Vinci's *The Last Supper,* Jesus sits at the center of the table with six disciples on one side and six on the other.

Also leading to longer life spans are advancements in the medical field at the level of cellular behavior. We will be able to heal illnesses such as cancer and autoimmune diseases by dealing with their source: cells that malfunction. In addition, we will identify a fine, etheric substance that binds cells to each other. This microscopic discovery will lead to a revolution in medicine, as it will allow us to positively manipulate the way in which cells relate to each other and react to outside influences.

— The feminine energy will become stronger and more powerful, bringing unity and healing to us all. We will begin to see increasing numbers of women as national leaders: the Divine feminine force will bring unity and harmony between the energies of the sexes.

— Barack Obama will be a one-term President.

— Future generations will be much more knowledgeable, especially in the sense that they will be connected to nature. The children of Earth will return to a dependency on, and respect for, the natural world.

— The future of medicine lies in natural healing through wholesome foods, the mind, light therapy, balancing our energy fields, and healing at the cellular level. We will witness amazing discoveries in health care, especially in regard to reducing the need to cut into the body so often by understanding the integrity of the body as a whole. Embryonic stem cells produced through therapeutic cloning will be integrated into future therapies.

— Humanity will travel in space and, in the distant future, we will each own our own airplane.

— Living creatures will visit us from other galaxies, but they won't be the frightening aliens we've seen in movies.

— We'll discover other planets and better understand the universe—specifically, how to work with it for our own benefit. However, we will do so through innovative means that aren't destructive. Further, a foreign planet will soon pass through our solar system, making for some very interesting encounters and supernatural occurrences.

— We'll identify life on other planets. We'll also relocate to other planets when the shift of the poles takes place. After this subsides, we'll return to Earth.

— We'll utilize more of the capacity of our brains and invent devices to connect to the next dimension: the realm of continuous time where souls live without bodies.

— Telepathy, teleportation, and the intuitive mind will be used as methods for connecting to each other and preventing events from happening.

As a result of these changes, life on Earth will be far more harmonious and peaceful. I know it's difficult to envision a world like this with our present perspective, but we're evolving our thinking and finally letting go of limitations. Look into the future and see us together. Start celebrating, and forget about the negative predictions, which are simply vestiges of an era of darkness. Let's step into the light—let's step into wholeliness!

ACKNOWLEDGMENTS

This book would have never come to life without the help of my sister-in-spirit, Colette Baron-Reid. I was so impressed by her amazing soul and generosity. I feel the same about Reid Tracy, and I am eternally grateful to him for the chance to be a Hay House author. I also can't begin to express gratitude to my amazing editor, Jill Kramer, for her vision and talent.

This book is dedicated to those who have taught me wholeliness: my mother, Sanda; my father, Victor; my beautiful husband, Virgil; my daughters Carmen and Florina; and my super-talented and gorgeous daughter Alexandra, who worked with me so hard to fulfill this project.

And last but certainly not least, this book would have never come to fruition without the brilliant efforts of my wonderful friend and editor, Nancy Peske.

•• ● ••

ABOUT THE AUTHOR

Best-selling author **Carmen Harra, Ph.D.**, is a clinical psychologist and TV personality who has been featured on an array of national shows, including *The View, Good Morning America,* and the *Today* show; and in publications such as *The New York Times,* the *New York Post,* and more.

Harra's extensive training in couples and cognitive therapy, combined with her uncanny intuitive abilities, has made her an internationally sought-after advisor who offers guidance to everyone from Hollywood celebrities to eminent politicians. She is also a talented musician with three CDs and has designed her own line of jewelry.

Visit her at: **www.CarmenHarra.com** and on Facebook at: **Carmen Harra: Wholeliness**.

•• ● ••

Hay House Titles of Related Interest

YOU CAN HEAL YOUR LIFE, the movie, starring Louise L. Hay & Friends
(available as a 1-DVD program and an expanded 2-DVD set)
Watch the trailer at: **www.LouiseHayMovie.com**

THE SHIFT, the movie,
starring Dr. Wayne W. Dyer
(available as a 1-DVD program and an expanded 2-DVD set)
Watch the trailer at: **www.DyerMovie.com**

•••

BE YOUR OWN SHAMAN:
Heal Yourself and Others with 21st-Century Energy Medicine,
by Deborah King

THE BODY "KNOWS": How to Tune In to Your Body
and Improve Your Health, by Caroline M. Sutherland

CHAKRA CLEARING: Awakening Your Spiritual Power
to Know and Heal (book-with-CD), by Doreen Virtue

DISSOLVING THE EGO, REALIZING THE SELF:
Contemplations from the Teachings of David R. Hawkins, M.D., Ph.D.,
edited by Scott Jeffrey (available August 2011)

THE MAP: Finding the Magic and Meaning in the Story of Your Life,
by Colette Baron-Reid

MENDING THE PAST AND HEALING THE FUTURE
WITH SOUL RETRIEVAL, by Alberto Villoldo, Ph.D.

THE POWER OF YOUR SPIRIT: A Guide to Joyful Living,
by Sonia Choquette

All of the above are available at your local bookstore,
or may be ordered by contacting Hay House (see next page).

•••

We hope you enjoyed this Hay House book.
If you'd like to receive our online catalog featuring additional information
on Hay House books and products, or if you'd like to find out more
about the Hay Foundation, please contact:

Hay House, Inc.,
P.O. Box 5100, Carlsbad, CA 92018-5100
(760) 431-7695 or (800) 654-5126
(760) 431-6948 (fax) or (800) 650-5115 (fax)
www.hayhouse.com® • **www.hayfoundation.org**

•••

Published and distributed in Australia by: Hay House Australia Pty. Ltd.,
18/36 Ralph St., Alexandria NSW 2015 • *Phone:* 612-9669-4299 •
Fax: 612-9669-4144 • www.hayhouse.com.au

Published and distributed in the United Kingdom by: Hay House UK, Ltd.,
292B Kensal Rd., London W10 5BE • *Phone:* 44-20-8962-1230 •
Fax: 44-20-8962-1239 • www.hayhouse.co.uk

Published and distributed in the Republic of South Africa by: Hay House SA
(Pty), Ltd., P.O. Box 990, Witkoppen 2068 • *Phone/Fax:* 27-11-467-8904 •
www.hayhouse.co.za

Published in India by: Hay House Publishers India, Muskaan Complex, Plot No.
3, B-2, Vasant Kunj, New Delhi 110 070 • *Phone:* 91-11-4176-1620 •
Fax: 91-11-4176-1630 • www.hayhouse.co.in

Distributed in Canada by: Raincoast, 9050 Shaughnessy St., Vancouver, B.C.
V6P 6E5 • *Phone:* (604) 323-7100 • *Fax:* (604) 323-2600 • www.raincoast.com

•••

Take Your Soul on a Vacation

Visit **www.HealYourLife.com®** to regroup, recharge, and reconnect
with your own magnificence. Featuring blogs, mind-body-spirit news,
and life-changing wisdom from Louise Hay and friends.

Visit **www.HealYourLife.com** today!